T0301637

Rethinking Work, Ageing and Retirement

Series Editors: **David Lain**, Newcastle University, **Sarah Vickerstaff**, University of Kent and **Mariska van der Horst**, Vrije Universiteit Amsterdam

This multidisciplinary series brings together researchers from a range of fields including management and organizational studies, gerontology, sociology, psychology and social policy, to explore the impact of extended working lives on older people and organizations.

Forthcoming in the series:

Rethinking Financial Behaviour;
Rationality and Resistance in the Financialization of Everyday Life
By **Ariane Agunsoye**

Out now in the series:

Older Workers in Transition;
European Experiences in a Neoliberal Era
Edited by **David Lain**, **Sarah Vickerstaff** and **Mariska van der Horst**

Find out more at

bristoluniversitypress.co.uk/
rethinking-work-ageing-and-retirement

Rethinking Work, Ageing and Retirement

Series Editors: **David Lain**, Newcastle University, **Sarah Vickerstaff**, University of Kent and **Mariska van der Horst**, Vrije Universiteit Amsterdam

Find out more at
bristoluniversitypress.co.uk/
rethinking-work-ageing-and-retirement

MENOPAUSE TRANSITIONS AND THE WORKPLACE

Theorizing Transitions,
Responsibilities and Interventions

Edited by
Vanessa Beck and Jo Brewis

BRISTOL
UNIVERSITY
PRESS

First published in Great Britain in 2024 by

Bristol University Press
University of Bristol
1–9 Old Park Hill
Bristol
BS2 8BB
UK
t: +44 (0)117 374 6645
e: bup-info@bristol.ac.uk

Details of international sales and distribution partners are available at bristoluniversitypress.co.uk

British Library Cataloguing in Publication Data
A catalogue record for this book is available from the British Library

ISBN 978-1-5292-1570-0 hardcover
ISBN 978-1-5292-1571-7 ePub
ISBN 978-1-5292-1572-4 ePdf

Cover design: Andrew Corbett
Front cover image: © Andrew Corbett
Bristol University Press use environmentally responsible print partners.
Printed and bound in Great Britain by CPI Group (UK) Ltd, Croydon, CR0 4YY

FSC
www.fsc.org
MIX
Paper | Supporting responsible forestry
FSC® C013604

For Andrea

Contents

Series Editors' Preface

David Lain, Sarah Vickerstaff and Mariska van der Horst

The 'Rethinking Work, Ageing and Retirement' book series explores the impact of extended working lives and changes to welfare states and labour markets on people, organizations and society. The radical changes affecting work and retirement were an impetus for the series. In particular, rising state pension ages, shifts towards individual responsibility and risk in private pensions saving, and the abolition of mandatory retirement ages in a number of countries now frame decisions about retirement. In theory, these policy developments extend individual discretion about continuing in employment, which may create new opportunities for those who want – and are able – to work. In practice, however, it arguably makes retirement timing only a hypothetical choice that people can be held more accountable for. Individuals must now assume greater financial responsibility for remaining in work as long as they need to. For significant numbers of older people this may be difficult to achieve, however, given evidence of widespread age discrimination in the labour market and reduced employment opportunities for this group. This is in addition to difficulties individuals experience in the labour market at any age – for example, due to racism or ableism, or constraints on time and energy stemming from outside paid work, such as care responsibilities. Work itself also appears to be getting more precarious, albeit to differing degrees across countries, and the management of older workers is becoming less straightforward given uncertainties around retirement.

It is in this context, we are delighted to welcome this excellent volume on menopause transitions and the workplace edited by Vanessa Beck and Jo Brewis. It is well established that health-related issues have a significant impact on whether people continue working up to, and beyond, pension ages. We also know, as the editors of this volume point out in their introduction, that over half of women will at some stage experience one or more severe symptom(s) of menopause and some will consider leaving work because of this. Despite this, menopause transitions in the workplace have only recently been recognized as an issue of importance within the academic and policy literature, and this was in part because of the significant work the editors and authors of this book have done on this topic. Importantly, the book moves beyond a purely biomedical focus, examining menopause as a biopsychosocial process that has importance for transitions in the workplace; flexible working; trade unions; spatial (in)justice; and male allyship. The book makes key theoretical and empirical contributions to both the topics explored in the book series and to the literature more generally.

List of Figures and Tables

Figures

Table

Notes on Contributors

Carol Atkinson is Professor of Human Resource Management and Director of Research, based in Manchester Metropolitan University Business School's Centre for Decent Work and Productivity. Her research focuses on creating high quality employment and is based around particular themes which include: gender, age and careers, particularly gender pay gaps and menopause in the workplace; job quality in adult social care; and people management and employment in small and medium-sized enterprises.

Hannah Bardett graduated with a first-class honours degree in Social and Public Policy and Business and Management from the University of Glasgow. She is currently on a graduate programme with the UK Government Civil Service Fast Stream, having previously worked as a Research Officer for a shared transport organization in the third sector.

Vanessa Beck is Professor in Employment Studies at the University of Bristol Business School. She is interested in individuals and groups at the margins of the labour market, including those who are unemployed or underemployed, and who experience multiple and complex barriers to (high quality) employment. She co-authored the UK Government Equalities Office report *The Effects of Menopause Transition on Women's Economics Participation in the UK* (2017), alongside Jo Brewis, Andrea Davies and Jesse Matheson. The team have also published on menopause as a workplace issue in outlets like *Organization, Climacteric, Human Resource Management Journal* (alongside Carol and Jo Duberley) and the *International Journal of Management Reviews.*

Jo Brewis is Professor of People and Organisations at The Open University Business School. She has a longstanding interest in bodies and organizations and was the lead author on the UK Government

Equalities Office report *The Effects of Menopause Transition on Women's Economics Participation in the UK* (2017), alongside Vanessa, Andrea Davies and Jesse Matheson. The team have also published on menopause as a workplace issue in outlets like *Organization, Climacteric, Human Resource Management Journal* (alongside Carol and Jo Duberley) and the *International Journal of Management Reviews.*

Jo Duberley is Professor of Organization Studies at the University of Birmingham. Central to her research is an interest in the concept of career. In recent years, she has developed research examining the impact of gender, ethnicity, social class and age on careers in a variety of contexts, including defence, professional service organizations and the police in the UK. Her current interests focus on the career progression of women in the professions, ageing and menopause at work.

Gavin Jack is Professor of Management in the Department of Management, Monash Business School, Melbourne. His research interests include postcolonial theory and analysis of management, organization and marketing topics, gender and diversity in the workplace, post-development theory and sustainable and equitable agriculture in the Global South. Gavin has published co-authored monographs and edited books as well as in journals including *Human Relations, Journal of Organizational Behavior* and *Academy of Management Review.* He is a former co-Chair of the Critical Management Studies Division of the Academy of Management; co-editor (with Nimruji Jammulamadaka) of the Springer book series *Managing the Post-Colony*; and (with Nimruji Jammulamadaka, Alex Faria and Shaun Ruggunan) co-guest editor of a special issue of *Organization* on decolonizing management and organizational knowledge.

Catrina Page is Lecturer in Organizational Behaviour and Human Resource Management at Manchester Metropolitan University in the Department of People and Performance. Her research interests include exploring the impact of work-based interventions that support mental well-being, resilience and productivity. She is currently researching and evaluating a menopause awareness training programme across a wide range of organizations.

Jane Parry is Associate Professor of Work and Employment in the University of Southampton Business School. A sociologist of work, her research looks at how employment and careers are changing within different occupations, as well as how disadvantage operates within labour markets and organizations. She led the cross-institutional UKRI/ESRC-funded project Work After Lockdown, which followed organizational learning around pandemic experiences, working closely with practice and policy communities. Its findings around hybrid and remote working have been widely cited in parliamentary publications from Westminster and the Senedd, and she has published in journals such as *Sociology, Work, Employment and Society* and *Gender, Work and Organization*. Jane recently sat on the Department of Business, Energy and Industrial Strategy's working group on The Future of Work, looking at their Area of Research Interest on flexible work, and in 2021 was the highest-ranking academic in *HR Magazine's* influential thinkers list. A former parliamentary academic fellow for the Parliamentary Office on Science and Technology, Jane undertook research there looking at skills development in policy careers. She has led research for the Advisory, Conciliation and Arbitration Service on managing flexible work in a post-pandemic landscape, and is driven by producing impactful research.

Kathleen Riach is Professor in Organizational Studies in the Adam Smith Business School at the University of Glasgow. Her work focuses on relationships between intersections of ageing, gender and the body and organizational subjectivities and modes of inequality. At the time of writing, Kathleen holds a British Academy Midcareer Fellowship and is writing a book developing a new organizational theory of ageing, based on a ten-year study of growing older at work. Alongside Gavin and Martha Hickey, she led the development of MIPO (Menopause Information Pack for Organizations), a free and open-access resource for line managers to support employees through menopause, which has been visited over 12,000 times across 52 countries. She is currently working with the Scottish government and NHS Scotland on a large survey exploring menopause and menstrual health in the workplace and has recently been invited to be a UK delegate for the G20 engagement group on gender equity, the W20.

Celia Roberts is Professor in the School of Sociology at the Australian National University, Canberra. She is currently working on an interdisciplinary project on the translation of epigenetics into antenatal care and completing a book about reproduction in climate crisis. Her previous books exploring the biosocial nature of embodiment, sex/gender and sexuality include *Puberty in Crisis: The Sociology of Early Sexual Development* (2015, Cambridge University Press), *Messengers of Sex: Hormones, Biomedicine and Feminism* (2007, Cambridge University Press) and, with Adrian Mackenzie and Maggie Mort, *Living Data: Making Sense of Health Biosensing* (2018, Bristol University Press).

Karen Throsby is Professor of Gender Studies in the School of Sociology and Social Policy at the University of Leeds. Her research explores the intersections of gender, health, technology across a range of sites including the new reproductive technologies, surgical weight management, endurance sport, and most recently, food. She is the author of *When IVF Fails: Feminist, Infertility and the Negotiation of Normality* (2004, Palgrave), *Immersion: Marathon Swimming, Embodiment and Identity* (2016, Manchester University Press) and *Sugar Rush: Science, Politics and the Demonisation of Fatness* (2023, Manchester University Press).

1

Introduction

Vanessa Beck and Jo Brewis

Why is menopause a workplace issue?

In focusing on menopausal women in the labour market and specific workplaces, this edited volume aims to re-theorize the management of people as it relates to the connections between gender, age and the body in organizations. The 'bodily turn' in management and organization studies is now nearing the end of its fourth decade (see, for early examples of this research, Burrell, 1984; Hearn et al, 1989; Acker, 1990; Brewis and Grey, 1994), and work which critically unpicks diversity initiatives dates back at least to the early 2000s (for example, Kersten, 2000; Lorbiecki and Jack, 2000; Dick and Cassell, 2002). Despite this, the menopause is still rarely discussed in management and organization studies, the sociology of work and employment literature or HRM research.

Menopause transitions encompass perimenopause where symptoms begin, through menopause which marks the day when a woman's periods have stopped for 12 months, to post-menopause thereafter, during which symptoms often continue. Symptoms can be both physical (for example, erratic periods, hot flushes, night sweats, insomnia and aches and pains) and psychological (for example, anxiety, irritability, loss of focus and forgetfulness). Research from the UK suggests that some 54 per cent of women will experience at least one severe symptom – that is, one that significantly affects their quality of life (Evandrou et al, 2021). That said, menopause is also unique to everyone that goes through it – as Karen Throsby and Celia Roberts establish in Chapter 2 in this volume, there is no such thing as THE menopause. One of the most common variations is premature menopause, defined as occurring before the age of 40, which is something 1 per cent of women experience. Menopause can also be precipitated by surgery – such as the removal of ovaries – or certain medications, like Tamoxifen which may be used to treat breast cancer.

Further, and importantly for our purposes here, menopause transitions have implications for work and are, in turn, affected by work. Indeed, and as we establish elsewhere (Atkinson et al, 2021a), this is a very important area for employers and academic researchers, given that:

• The global north workforce is ageing, and older women have been one of the fastest growing groups among this workforce.
• There are legal frameworks (for example, the UK Equality Act, 2010) which protect against discrimination including on the basis of sex and age: to date there have been five successful menopause-based employment tribunals in the UK.
• Women experiencing menopause transition may consider leaving work altogether and losing their experience and expertise is costly for employers (incurring direct and indirect costs of replacement), with some tacit knowledge lost for good.
• In order to be a good employer with decent employment relations, managers at all levels need to be aware of menopause issues, be able to discuss them, and provide appropriate support where necessary.

In this editorial introduction, we review progress to date in workplace practice and academic research in this area, and provide an overview of how the chapters in the volume speak to some of the existing gaps in our knowledge.

Before we continue, we should also note that 'woman', 'women', 'she', 'her', 'female' and so on are used in the main as placeholders in this chapter and throughout the volume. This is because anyone who has ovaries, including some transgender men and other gender-diverse people, will experience menopause – not just cis women. Karen Throsby and Celia Roberts make this argument very clearly and in more depth in the next chapter.

Where is workplace practice in this area now?

In the global north, and the UK especially, there has in fact been a huge groundswell of interest in issues related to menopause in the workplace since the late 2010s. As editors of this book, we have been acutely aware of this since our report for the Government Equalities Office was published (Brewis et al, 2017). This examined the effects of menopause transition on women's economic participation in the UK and was based on a systematic evidence review of existing literature, specifically 104 English language publications dating from the beginning of January 1990 to the end of March 2016.

At the time the report was published, there was only a handful of organizations in the UK who took menopause seriously as a workplace issue. It was poorly understood in the context of both wider society and employment, even somewhat of a taboo due to what Jack et al (2014) refer to as gendered ageism. This is the intersection of sexist attitudes towards women and stereotyping of people in mid-life and older age. As such, the prevailing climate certainly reflected Jack et al's argument that mid-life women at work were unsupported around menopause and felt side-lined, invisible, even unwelcome.

Looking back over the ensuing period of time, the situation today – in the UK at least – is significantly different. Very important work has been undertaken by consultancies like Henpicked: Menopause in the Workplace (nd) and their sister organization the Menopause Friendly Accreditation (nd) – both of whom we have been lucky enough to work with over the years. The same is true of awareness raising by women in the public eye including Davina McCall, Mariella Frostrup, Louise Minchin and Meg Mathews and, more recently, reports from the Women and Equalities Committee (WEC, 2022) and the All-Party Parliamentary Group on Menopause (APPGM, 2022), following championing by MPs including Carolyn Harris and Caroline Nokes. There are also prominent actors in this space who advocate a natural approach to managing menopause symptoms, particularly by following a specific diet and taking supplements, such as Dr Marilyn Glenville and Maryon Stewart.

Professional and advocacy organizations have been equally active in this space. These include:

- Advance HE (Brewis, 2020);
- the Advisory, Conciliation and Arbitration Service (2022);
- the British Medical Society, the Royal College of Gynaecologists, the Royal College of General Practitioners, the Faculty of Sexual and Reproductive Health, the Faculty of Occupational Medicine and the Faculty of Public Health (Hamoda et al, 2021);

- Business in the Community (2022);
- the Chartered Institute of Personnel and Development (2022);
- NHS Employers (2020);
- sectoral skill bodies (Standard Chartered and Financial Services Skills Commission, 2021);
- and a wide range of trade unions and union confederations (see, for example, GMB, nd; NASUWT, nd; UNISON, nd; Wales TUC Cymru, 2017).

The same is true of many mid-life women workers who have campaigned tirelessly for menopause to be placed on the agenda in their organizations; and their employers who have taken up the baton internally but in some cases also done outreach work across their sectors to spread the word. The Labour Party (2019) have, further, pledged to ensure that employers provide flexible working arrangements for women transitioning through menopause if it gains power – although of course this kind of set up won't necessarily benefit those in jobs where only very limited forms of flexibility are available and/or women for whom reduced hours arrangements like part-time work are not easy to sustain economically.

UK society and UK workplaces are therefore now far more attuned to menopause as a mainly natural and normal phase of life for women. This is obvious when we consider that a survey we ran in summer 2018 in conjunction with TUC Education (n = 5,399) indicated that menopause guidelines or policies existed in only 10 per cent of organizations (Beck, Brewis and Davies 2020, 2021). Comparing this to recent data published by the Chartered Institute of Personnel and Development (2022, p 3), their estimate is that 30 per cent of UK employers now provide support of this kind – a tripling of the original numbers in just four years. As suggested previously, organizations across the private, public and third sectors have made enormous progress on this front, exemplified by case studies on the Henpicked: Menopause in the Workplace and The Menopause Friendly Accreditation websites. And, in September 2022, the first Menopause Friendly Employers Awards ceremony was held in London, with ten categories, and is now an annual event.

Where is academic knowledge in this area now?

Academic research has also moved on considerably since our government report was published. We now know more about some of the gaps we identified then. To begin with, there is additional research which evaluates workplace interventions around menopause. For example, Hardy et al (2018a) report the success of a self-help cognitive behaviour therapy manual used by working women struggling with hot flushes and night sweats. Those taking part reported reduced symptoms, less problematic symptoms, better sleep, less impact on work and an improved attitude to menopause per se. Similarly, Verburgh et al (2020) look at a work-life programme designed for mid-life women in low paid jobs in a Dutch hospital. Their findings show that this programme had a positive ameliorative effect on these women's menopausal symptoms. Hardy, Griffiths and Hunter (2019a) also wrote a short online training package for managers around menopause. This was intended to be educational and attitude–changing as well as improving their confidence to support menopausal colleagues at work. It was extremely well received by those who trialled it.

There are, in addition, now studies which feature the voices of working menopausal women beyond those in professional and managerial occupations. One example is Verburgh et al's (2020) Dutch research as cited earlier. Yoeli, Macnaughton and McLusky (2021) have published a metareview of women's experiences in casual, informal or precarious jobs. Moreover, Riach and Jack's (2021) survey across universities and healthcare organizations in Australia includes respondents holding administrative posts in higher education as well as nurses, healthcare assistants and those providing care in domestic settings.

Equally, more studies featuring data from the UK have been published since 2017, when they constituted just 19 per cent of the evidence base.[1] The increase here is actually marked and includes the Hardy et al (2018a, Hardy, Griffiths and Hunter, 2019a) papers indexed previously. Evandrou et al (2021) and Bryson et al (2022), which we discuss next, also fall into this category. The same is true of our aforementioned research discussing the results from the TUC Education survey (Beck et al, 2020, 2021). Atkinson et al (2021b) report data from their survey of female police officers, staff and volunteers; and Hardy, Griffiths and Hunter's (2019b), Butler's (2020) and Steffan's (2021; Steffan and Potočnik, 2023) research was based on qualitative interviews with UK respondents. Bodza, Morrey and Hogan's (2019) data also came from qualitative interviews with a small sample of UK counsellors. Hardy, Griffiths and Hunter (2017, Hardy et al, 2018b), on the other hand, rely on UK survey data to discuss what mid-life women workers want from their employers and managers around menopause; and its effects on their working lives.

Studies acknowledging that menopause transition at work can be positive are also more common now. Jack, Riach and Bariola (2019), for example, draw on interview data from university staff in Australia to conclude that some women felt they knew themselves and their bodies better as well as developing more creativity and resourcefulness due to menopause. In addition, they talked about not feeling the pressure to look sexually attractive or be subservient at work any longer, as well as sensing an obligation to discuss menopause at work to make life easier for younger women in future. Relatedly, Butler's (2020) local government participants developed very strong collective bonds during their transitions, which they reported meant they were much better able to cope with any attendant challenges at work and elsewhere as a result. These women also talked about resisting the biomedical discourse of decline and failure around menopause, something which is discussed at length in Throsby and Roberts in this volume.

In addition, two studies speaking to the economic cost of menopause transition, along both the extensive margin which is associated with leaving work and the intensive margin which focuses on the costs connected with staying at work, are now available. Both draw on longitudinal data from the UK National Childhood Development Study (NCDS), and as such also contribute to filling another gap in the evidence base, which hitherto was dominated by cross-sectional research. In addition, these studies add to our knowledge around the relationship between continued employment and menopause. The first is Evandrou et al (2021) who use successive waves of the NCDS to find that women reporting problematic menopausal symptoms at age 50 were much more likely to have either left work altogether or to have reduced their hours by age 55 than those who did not. The second is Bryson et al (2022) who use a similar methodology to conclude that women who experience early menopause, i.e., before the age of 45[2], and/ or women who have psychological symptoms have lower employment rates as they enter their 50s than their counterparts.

As such, and because of the demographic, business, legal and social responsibility cases for employers to pay attention to menopause and intervene accordingly, as outlined at the outset of this chapter, there is a good deal to celebrate at the time of writing. But there is also still a great deal to be done. On the policy and practice front, we know that small and medium sized enterprises are less likely to have menopause support in place. Equally, the 2022 WEC and APPG reports draw attention to the need, among other things, for section 14 of the Equality Act (2010) to come into force. This would mean a claim of dual direct discrimination on the basis of a combination of two protected characteristics (for example, sex and age in the case of menopause) can be brought. An additional recommendation was for the government to consult on the introduction of menopause as an additional protected characteristic in this Act, alongside pregnancy and maternity. The creation of a government Menopause Ambassador to support employers is a third recommendation, which is related to a fourth, as follows:

> The Government must update and promote guidance for employers on best practice menopause at work policies and supporting interventions. This should include the economic justification and productivity benefits of doing so and be tailored to organisations of different sizes and resources to ensure it is as effective as possible. (APPG, 2022, p 13)

We revisit the government's response to the WEC report in the conclusion to this volume. As for academic research, the volume at hand will add to the still relatively small knowledge base in this space as we explain next.

Outline of this volume

The next chapter in this volume is titled 'Bodies of Change: Menopause as Biopsychosocial Process' by Karen Throsby and Celia Roberts. In a discussion which sets the theoretical and conceptual tone for the whole book, Karen and Celia begin with the observation that it is only humans and two species of whale who go through menopause and that they are also the only living beings who survive beyond their reproductive years. Unlike killer whales in particular, who are vital to their pod's survival after menopause, the same phenomenon in humans is still understood in the prevailing biomedical discourse as a period of decline, failure, loss and ending. As Karen and Celia point out, this construction limits not just the questions we can ask about menopause but also the ways we answer those questions. They argue that menopause in human beings who are assigned female at birth has been pathologized since the 1950s. Instead, they suggest, we need to understand it through a biopsychosocial[3] lens and specifically as a transition. Menopause is, as they point out, not a catastrophic ending or solely biological but an experience that is significantly inflected by an individual's social context and their psyche.

Looking at menopause this way, Karen and Celia aver, also allows us to move beyond the biomedical insistence that women are woefully uneducated about it, necessitating concerted awareness raising, pharmaceutical interventions (that is, hormone replacement therapy) and lifestyle changes. They suggest this lack of education is actually an unlikely scenario which overlooks the hormonal and technological interventions we are all used to in what they call the age of biological control and its imperatives to live as healthy a life as possible, especially aimed at those assigned female at birth. Karen and Celia go on to suggest that we need to consider whose bodies count in the prevailing discourse and ensuing policy and practice around menopause, and that the bodies of those who are LGBTQI+, have disabilities, experience premature menopause and/ or are childless (whether by choice or not) are largely if not entirely absent.

Indeed if, Karen and Celia suggest, decades of feminist theorizing have taught us that our bodies are not in any way separate from the worlds we inhabit, then there is no one thing that we can refer to as THE menopause. By attending to more diverse experiences, we can then pose questions like 'How do those identifying as LGBTQI+ feel about menopausal hormonal changes widely decried as problematic because they are "de-gendering" (such as increased facial hair)?' (Throsby and Roberts, this volume, Chapter 2). Moreover, bodies do not simply change during this life phase, but have the capacity to change their worlds. Since, Karen and Celia conclude,

> existing research tends to repeat well-worn stories of loss and decline, (re)producing menopause as something to be dreaded and treated, and framing those who refuse treatment as woefully ignorant[, i]t is time to break out of this circular trap, to listen more carefully to people's experiences and to create new stories. (Throsby and Roberts, this volume, Chapter 2)

Next comes 'Exploring menopause transition in the workplace' by Carol Atkinson, Jo Duberley and Catrina Page. This chapter is one of two that focus specifically on organizational practice, workplace interventions and possibilities for further provisions in this area, here with a particular focus on evaluating (potential) employer interventions. It is based on UK survey data gathered from a range of sectors, thus further addressing aspects of the aforementioned dearth of knowledge about the UK context. Moreover, with over 5,000 responses and a combination of closed and open-ended questions, these data provide a methodological breadth which has not been common so far. The data also extend the evaluation of menopausal interventions to considerations of what works for respondents, as well as foregrounding others' responses to colleagues experiencing menopause in the workplace, another area which was largely invisible in the publications we reviewed for our 2017 government report.

The chapter draws on a psychological contract framework and considers (and updates) our knowledge on the experience of menopause at work as it relates to the impact it has on working, as well as the compensations that are undertaken by those experiencing it to 'overcome difficulties' (Atkinson, Duberley and Page, this volume, Chapter 3). This is linked to disclosure; embarrassment; the fear of discrimination and workplace incivility; attempts to normalize the conversation around menopause; the role of line managers in these processes; and, overall, to help and support those in transition at work. The psychological contract lens allows Carol, Jo and Catrina to pull these issues together to consider the overall implications for the employment relationship. Cross-tabulating organizational and line managers' support with women's willingness to disclose highlights the shared responsibility to create workplaces in which meaningful help and support around menopause can be provided.

This leads Carol, Jo and Catrina to conclude with the call that 'substantial cultural change is needed to normalize the conversation around menopause' (Chapter 3). Their work shows how central such menopause support is for anything from organizational commitment, via job satisfaction, turnover intentions, organizational citizenship behaviour, and in-role performance, all the way to well-being. The breadth of this list reinforces the final challenge voiced in this chapter: that organizations ignore this at their peril.

Then we move to Jane Parry's chapter 'Workplace Policies, Menopause and Flexible Working: The Need for a More Collective Approach'. Jane's chapter considers the poor fit between workplace policy, and in particular flexible working, and menopausal experiences. It is also based on UK data and again draws on considerations based on the psychological contract as well as evaluating organizational interventions around menopause. However, and importantly, Jane's chapter clarifies that this is about psychological contract fulfilment rather than breach, given that there are still relatively few workplaces with well-established menopause provisions. Alongside the previous chapter by Carol, Jo and Catrina, which is based on similar conceptions, a theme emerges here that demonstrates the personal side of the two-way relationship between menopause and work: just as menopause symptoms affect work and work affects symptoms, so do individuals within workplaces interact. Without a supportive network of colleagues and understanding line managers, menopause in the workplace can become a serious issue that may, ultimately, lead to the withdrawal of experienced women from the workplace. However, Jane's chapter is testament to how preventable such an outcome is.

Jane highlights the importance of responsive organizational offers in this space and in particular the benefits of well-designed and monitored flexible working arrangements. This is done by differentiating between different areas that (potentially) influence, are beneficial or a hindrance to such flexible working arrangements, including: the visibility of menopause in organizations' HRM discussions; the triggers that prompt employers to get involved in menopause as a workplace issue; the different approaches that organizations are adopting; the adaptive potential of flexible work in supporting employees around menopause; and learnings from the COVID-19 pandemic that can be applied to work organization around menopause experiences. The key argument that the chapter promotes is summarized as follows:

> while informal and idiosyncratic approaches to managing flexible working arrangements have been presented in organizations as a suitable approach for managing diverse and fluctuating workforce needs, there is a potential deficiency in relying upon this kind of psychological contract around menopause. Idiosyncratic approaches neglect to engage with the challenge of reconciling the lack of a dialogue around this issue in many organizations and the sensitivity that is still experienced in raising menopause experiences with line managers. It is argued that shifting back towards a psychological contract with more clearly defined terms and understandings for both parties will be more beneficial at this early stage of embedding good practice around menopause workforce support. (Parry, this volume, Chapter 4)

Importantly, this highlights how existing approaches to providing menopause support may exclude the individuals who may feel most vulnerable as a result of their experiences and therefore feel unable to discuss their situation with their line manager. At the same time, Jane makes suggestions around a more clearly defined psychological contract that would help to address these issues and create a supportive employment context around changing working needs related to menopause transitions.

Vanessa's chapter 'Menopause and Trade Unions' is our sixth chapter. Again it is based on UK data gathered as part of our TUC Education survey and elsewhere and draws out findings from these data as they relate directly to trade union activities and trade union members as well as evaluating workplace interventions. Trade unions themselves assert that menopause in the workplace is a trade union issue, which they are increasingly willing to tackle as we have suggested earlier in this chapter. Taking a union lens to consider menopause issues in workplaces also has the advantage that a broad range of sectoral and occupational contexts can be investigated. Our data provide insights into, for example, public services (UNISON), construction and manufacturing (Unite), engineering and managers (Prospect), nurses (Royal College of Nursing), retail (GMB) and education (University and College Union). Vanessa compares our TUC Education survey data with four other data sets: a survey taking place after menopause awareness workshops for union representatives that we ran as part of the TUC Education project; qualitative data from interviews with representatives who attended the workshops; and data from two surveys sent to staff in a local council. These data taken together show that raising awareness among trade unionists leads to an increase in conversations about menopause, and that a more diverse group of individuals, including cis men, are participating in these conversations.

The chapter also draws two broader conclusions about the role of menopause in trade union work. The first is that the engagement that trade union representatives stimulate and encourage around menopause shows the relevance and importance of the trade union movement to diverse workforces. Following periods of at times volatile and turbulent union membership, this means that such engagement with the still partially taboo subject of menopause can be utilized as part of a trade union renewal strategy. Second, and relatedly, Vanessa argues that addressing the needs of individuals experiencing menopause transition at work can lead to improvements in employment and working conditions overall. Many of the workplace adjustments recommended to address menopause transitions, such as availability of drinking water, control over temperature regulation, addressing working times and the intensity of work at certain times, would benefit most members of staff. Vanessa thus concludes that

> [t]he two arguments are co-dependent in that increasing social awareness of menopause and of trade union activity in this field would make for greater union leverage to ensure broader workplace change. In addition, both sit within a broader understanding of employment relations and collegiality which benefits from solidarity among and between workforces. (Beck, this volume, Chapter 5)

This is followed by Jo's chapter 'Spatial (In)Justice and Hot Flushes in the Workplace: Some Musings and Provocations'. This is also based on data gathered in the UK and as such contributes to the aforementioned gap in the knowledge base. In addition, it draws on accounts from women in a wide range of occupations, many of which are not professional or managerial. Here Jo draws on our TUC Education survey data as well as data she gathered via surveys and semi-structured interviews at Northshire, a pseudonymous NHS hospital trust. She develops an argument around shared space at work and the common menopausal symptom of hot flushes. Open plan offices and other communal work areas are often, as Jo points out, 'beset with tensions around temperature and ventilation as a result' (Brewis, this volume, Chapter 6) of these symptoms. Many women are not as fortunate as journalist and television presenter Louise Minchin, who was able to negotiate with her BBC colleagues to have the thermostat in the studio where she presented the flagship breakfast programme turned down when she was working so it stayed 'super cool' (cited in Brewis, this volume, Chapter 6). We also know that high temperatures and poor ventilation can make the experience of hot flushes at work more unpleasant; and extant data suggest they are one of the main symptoms which make work more challenging.

With this context in place, Jo moves to analyse the survey and interview data through a lens provided by Philippopoulos-Mihalopoulos' concept of spatial justice and Watson's application of this concept to the Muslim practice of wudu, 'the ritual washing of head, neck, hands, arms and feet before prayer' (Brewis, this volume, Chapter 6), in public places. Philippopoulos-Mihalopoulos begins from the premise that human beings very frequently share the same physical space and thus that spatial justice is rooted in '*the conflict between bodies that are moved by a desire to occupy the same space at the same time ...* the emergence of a negotiation between bodies' (2015, p 3). Arguments between workers experiencing hot flushes and those who don't over how high a thermostat should be set, whether desktop fans are permissible in an open plan office and whether windows and doors should be open or closed speak to precisely this conflict. Some of this is regulated by organizational policies and regulations, like the requirement that all portable electrical appliances in use at work (such as fans) are regularly tested. But, as Philippopoulos-Mihalopoulos points out, these regulations are enacted, or resisted, by bodies in what he calls the lawscape. Moreover, negotiations about spatial justice are not just verbal but also corporeal, like shutting a window or turning a thermostat up in the case of the workplace. And, as Watson's analysis emphasizes, spatial justice 'is not an interaction between or negotiation of equals' (Brewis, this volume, Chapter 6). This is also illustrated in the data Jo deploys, for example in scenarios where managers refuse requests from staff for environmental adjustments like fans.

Jo's analysis moves somewhat beyond Philippopoulos-Mihalopoulos in presenting arguments around how lawscapes can be over-interpreted by those in authority especially so as to impose regulations in ways not intended by the authors of said regulations, and the way in which custom and practice at work can settle into patterns of inequality. She concludes by emphasizing Philippopoulos-Mihalopoulos' point that our 'shared world' has 'physical limits', pointing to the 'broader implications of [the concept of spatial justice] for menopause as an organizational issue and employment relations more generally' (Brewis, this volume, Chapter 6).

The final substantive chapter in this volume is 'Menopause and the Possibilities of Male Allyship' by Hannah Bardett, Kathleen Riach and Gavin Jack. Again it draws on empirical data from the UK. These data comprise of two sets of qualitative interviews with young cis men who had either just completed their undergraduate studies or were about to, all of whom held ambitions to move into professional and/ or managerial jobs, punctuated by conversations with their mothers about menopause at work. It also adds to our knowledge in terms of how others at work react to colleagues experiencing difficulties relating to menopause symptoms as well as reflecting on the possible challenges of relying on conversations between potential allies and those with lived experience as a basis for allyship. The chapter has two key foci, as follows:

First, to shed light on menopause equality work as a relational phenomenon based on the perspectives of a sample of male respondents. And second, to consider the prospective possibilities and challenges for men to act as workplace allies for working women going through menopause and to promote inclusive workplace environments. (Bardett, Riach and Jack, this volume, Chapter 7)

As Hannah, Kathleen and Gavin point out, allyship is far from being one thing, so they focused on what it might mean around menopause at work for their respondents. They contextualize their argument by pointing out that bottom-up action in organizations, which we referenced above, is common but carries with it risks around sustainability as well as additional labour for the women involved. At the opposite end, there is also a champions model whereby senior staff take on the role of advocating for and supporting menopausal colleagues as well as educating others. This, however, is potentially problematic if the consequence for senior men in particular is that they fall into tropes around heroic male saviours who also expect appreciation from the women they support. In between lies the possibility of allyship, which Madson et al define as follows:

being part of the dominant group, which provides allies with the ability to draw on social capital not available to marginalised individuals that can then be leveraged to create equity for marginalised groups. (cited in Bardett, Riach and Jack, this volume, Chapter 7)

Hannah, Gavin and Kathleen's findings suggest, on the positive side, that their young male respondents were very aware that menopause is not simply a biological phenomenon – per Karen and Celia's emphasis on the biopsychocultural model as outlined in Chapter 2. These young men also accepted that it was their responsibility to become more educated about menopause at work in particular. On the more contentious side, the respondents also identified tensions in advocating for people based on an experience they themselves could only ever approximate. They also found the question of who should be doing the necessary education a tricky one as well as suggesting that 'how, and where, to publicly acknowledge and engage with menopause as an issue of workplace inequality' was a difficult issue (Bardett, Riach and Jack, this volume, Chapter 7).

Finally, our editorial conclusion summarizes the volume's key messages and establishes a clear research agenda to follow going forward around menopause in the workplace.

Before we move on to Karen and Celia's chapter, we would like to sincerely thank all of our contributors for their patience and understanding with us while we worked to put this volume together, with the COVID-19 pandemic as a backdrop during most of this process. They have made a challenging process as enjoyable and straightforward as it could have been! We also very much hope that readers find the book interesting and thought-provoking and that it encourages you to undertake – or progress – your own research and/ or practice in this important area.

Notes

1. The empirical UK evidence base as reviewed in our 2017 report included studies done by or on behalf of the Trade Unions Congress (Paul, 2003; Trades Union Congress, 2014), by individual trade unions (the former National Union of Teachers, 2014), by third sector organizations (Social Issues Research Centre, 2002) and by academic teams led by Professor Amanda Griffiths at the University of Nottingham (Griffiths et al, 2006; Griffiths, MacLennan and Wong, 2010; Griffiths, MacLennan and Hassard, 2013).
2. For clarity, premature menopause is defined clinically as occurring before the age of 40, whereas early menopause is before the age of 45.
3. Also known as the biopsychocultural lens or approach.

References

Acker, J. (1990) 'Hierarchies, jobs, bodies: A theory of gendered organizations', *Gender & Society*, 4(2): 139–58.

Advisory, Conciliation and Arbitration Service (2022) 'Menopause at work', [online] 25 March. Available from: https://www.acas.org.uk/menopause-at-work [Accessed 17 November 2022].

All-Party Parliamentary Group on Menopause (APPG) (2022) *Inquiry to Assess the Impacts of Menopause and the Case for Policy Reform. Concluding Report*, [online] 12 October. Available from: https://menopause-appg. co.uk/wp-content/uploads/2022/10/APPG-Menopause-Inquiry-Concluding-Report-12.10.22-1.pdf (menopause-appg.co.uk) [Accessed 17 November 2022].

Atkinson, C., Beck, V., Brewis, J., Davies, A. and Duberley, J. (2021a) 'Menopause and the workplace: New directions in HRM research and HR practice', *Human Resource Management Journal*, 31(1): 49–64.

Atkinson, C., Carmichael, F. and Duberley, J. (2021b) 'The menopause taboo: examining women's embodied experiences of menopause in the UK police service', *Work, Employment and Society*, 35(4): 657–76.

Beck, V., Brewis, J. and Davies, A. (2020) 'The remains of the taboo: Experiences, attitudes, and knowledge about menopause in the workplace', *Climacteric*, 23(2): 158–64.

Beck, V., Brewis, J. and Davies, A. (2021) 'Women's experiences of menopause at work and performance management', *Organization*, 28(3): 510–520.

Bodza, C., Morrey, T. and Hogan, K.F. (2019) 'How do counsellors having menopausal symptoms experience their client work[?]: An interpretative phenomenological analysis', *Counselling and Psychotherapy Research*, 19(4): 544–52.

Brewis, J. (2020) *Menopause Awareness and Higher Education*, [online] 29 October. Available from: https://www.gov.uk/government/publications/menopause-transition-effects-on-womens-economic-participation [Accessed 17 November 2022].

Brewis, J., Beck, V., Davies, A. and Matheson, J. (2017) *The Impact of Menopause Transition on Women's Economic Participation in the UK*, [online] 20 July. Available from: https://menopauseintheworkplace.co.uk/wp-content/uploads/2020/04/menopause_report.pdf [Accessed 17 November 2022].

Brewis, J. and Grey, C. (1994) 'Re-eroticizing the organization: An exegesis and critique', *Gender, Work and Organization*, 1(2): 67–82.

Bryson, A., Conti, G., Hardy, G., Hardy, R., Peycheva, D. and Sullivan, A. (2022) 'The consequences of early menopause and menopause symptoms for labour market participation', *Social Science & Medicine*, 293, 114676.

Burrell, G. (1984) 'Sex and organizational analysis', *Organization Studies*, 5(2): 97–118.

Butler, C. (2020) 'Managing the menopause through "abjection work": When boobs can become embarrassingly useful, again', *Work, Employment and Society* 34(4): 696–712.

Business in the Community (2022) *Menopause in the Workplace*, [online] 3 October. Available from: https://www.bitc.org.uk/toolkit/menopause-in-the-workplace/ [Accessed 17 November 2022].

Chartered Institute of Personnel and Development (2022) *The Menopause at Work: A Guide for People Professionals*, [online] 9 August. Available from: https://www.cipd.org/en/knowledge/guides/menopause-people-professionals-guidance/ [Accessed 17 November 2022].

Dick, P. and Cassell, C. (2002) 'Barriers to managing diversity in a UK constabulary: The role of discourse', *Journal of Management Studies*, 39(7): 953–76.

Evandrou, M., Falkingham, J., Qin, M. and Vlachantoni, A. (2021) 'Menopausal transition and change in employment: Evidence from the National Child Development Study', *Maturitas*, 143(Jan): 96–104.

GMB (nd) 'Smash the stigma. Menopause in the workplace', [online]. Available from: https://www.gmb.org.uk/menopause/ [Accessed 17 November 2022].

Griffiths, A., Cox, S., Griffiths, R. and Wong, V. (2006) *Women Police Officers: Ageing, Work & Health*, report for the British Association of Women Police Officers, [online]. Available from: https://www.bawp.org/wp-content/uploads/2019/06/Ageing-Police-Officers.pdf [Accessed 22 May 2023].

Griffiths. A., MacLennan, S. and Wong, Y.Y.V. (2010) *Women's Experience of Working Through the Menopause*, report for the British Occupational Health Research Foundation, [online] December. Available from: BOHRF_Menopause_and_Work__Final_Report_Dec_2010 [Accessed 22 May 2023].

Griffiths A, MacLennan, S.J. and Hassard, J. (2013) 'Menopause and work: An electronic survey of employees' attitudes in the UK', *Maturitas*, 76(2): 155–9.

Hamoda, H., Morris, E., Marshall, M., Kasliwal, A., de Bono, A. and Rae, M. (2021) 'BMS, RCOG, RCGP, FSRH, FOM and FPH Position Statement in response to the BMA report "Challenging the culture on menopause for doctors" – August 2020', *Post Reproductive Health*, 27(2): 123–5.

Hardy, C., Griffiths. A. and Hunter, M.S. (2017) 'What do working menopausal women want? A qualitative investigation into women's perspectives on employer and line manager support', *Maturitas*, 101: 37–41.

Hardy, C., Griffiths, A., Norton, S. and Hunter, M.S. (2018a) 'Self-help cognitive behavior therapy for working women with problematic hot flushes and night sweats (MENOS@Work): A multicenter randomized controlled trial', *Menopause*, 25(5): 508–19.

Hardy, C., Thorne, E., Griffiths, A. and Hunter, M. (2018b) 'Work outcomes in midlife women: The impact of menopause, work stress and working environment', *Women's Midlife Health*, 4(3). doi: 0.1186/s40695-018-0036-z.

Hardy, C., Griffiths, A. and Hunter, M. (2019a) 'Development and evaluation of online menopause awareness training for line managers in UK organizations', *Maturitas*, 120(February): 83–9.

Hardy, C., Griffiths, A., Thorne, E. and Hunter, M. (2019b) 'Tackling the taboo: Talking menopause-related problems at work', *International Journal of Workplace Health Management*, 12(1): 28–38.

Hearn, J., Sheppard, D.L., Tancred-Sheriff, P. and Burrell, G. (eds) (1989) *The Sexuality of Organization*, London: Sage.

Henpicked: Menopause in the Workplace (nd) [online]. Available from: https://menopauseintheworkplace.co.uk/ [Accessed 17 November 2022].

Jack, G., Pitts, M., Riach, K., Bariola, E., Schapper, J. and Sarrel, P. (2014) *Women, Work and the Menopause: Releasing the Potential of Older Professional Women*, [online], September. Available from: https://apo.org.au/node/41511 [Accessed 20 July 2022].

Jack, G., Riach, K. and Bariola, E. (2019) 'Temporality and gendered agency: Menopausal subjectivities in women's work', *Human Relations*, 72(1): 122–43.

Kersten, A. (2000) 'Diversity management: Dialogue, dialectics and diversion', *Journal of Organizational Change Management*, 13(3): 235–48.

Labour Party (2019) 'Labour announces plans to break the stigma of the menopause at work', 20 September. No longer available online.

Lorbiecki, A. and Jack, G. (2000) 'Critical turns in the evolution of diversity management', *British Journal of Management*, 11(s1): S17–S31.

The Menopause Friendly Accreditation (nd) [online]. Available from: https://menopausefriendly.co.uk/ [Accessed 17 November 2022].

NASUWT (nd) *Menopause Policy*, [online]. Available from: Model Menopause Policy (nasuwt.org.uk) [Accessed 17 November 2022].

National Union of Teachers (2014) *Teachers Working Through the Menopause, Guidance for Members in England and Wales*, December. No longer available online.

NHS Employers (2020) 'Guidance on menopause at work', [online] 9 March. Available from: https://www.nhsemployers.org/publications/guidance-menopause-work [Accessed 17 November 2022].

Paul, J. (2003) *Working Through the Change: Health and Safety and the Menopause*, report for the Trades Union Congress, March. No longer available online.

Philippopoulos-Mihalopoulos, A. (2015) *Spatial Justice: Body, Lawscape, Atmosphere*, Oxford, New York: Routledge.

Riach, K. and Jack, G. (2021) 'Women's health in/and work: Menopause as an intersectional experience', *International Journal of Environmental Research and Public Health*, 18(20). doi: 10.3390/ijerph182010793.

Social Issues Research Centre (2002) *Jubilee Women. Fiftysomething Women – Lifestyle and Attitudes Now and Fifty Years Ago*, report for HRT Aware, [online]. Available from: http://www.sirc.org/publik/jubilee_women.pdf [Accessed 22 May 2023].

Standard Chartered and Financial Services Skills Commission (2021) *Menopause in the Workplace: Impact on Women in Financial Services*, [online] October. Available from: https://wp.financialservicesskills.org/wp-content/uploads/2021/11/Menopause-in-the-Workplace-Impact-on-Women-in-Financial-Services.pdf [Accessed 17 November 2022].

Steffan, B. (2021) 'Managing menopause at work: The contradictory nature of identity talk', *Gender, Work and Organization*, 28(1):195–214.

Steffan, B. and Potočnik, C. (2023) 'Thinking outside Pandora's box: Revealing differential effects of coping with physical and psychological menopause symptoms at work', *Human Relations*, 76(8): 1191–1225. Epub ahead of print. doi: 10.1177/00187267221089469.

Trades Union Congress (2014) *Age Immaterial: Women over 50 in the Workplace*, [online] February. Available from: https://www.tuc.org.uk/sites/default/files/Age_Immaterial_Women_Over_50_Report_2014_LR.pdf [Accessed 22 May 2023].

UNISON (nd) *The Menopause is a Workplace Issue: Guidance and Model Policy*, [online]. Available from: https://www.unison.org.uk/content/uploads/2019/10/25831.pdf [Accessed 17 November 2022].

Verburgh, M., Verdonk, P., Appelman, Y., Brood-van Zanten, M. and Nieuwenhuijsen, K. (2020) '"I get that spirit in me" – mentally empowering workplace health promotion for female workers in low-paid jobs during menopause and midlife', *International Journal of Environmental Research and Public Health*, 17(18): 6462.

Wales TUC Cymru (2017) *The Menopause in the Workplace: A Toolkit for Trade Unionists*, [online]. Available from: https://www.tuc.org.uk/menopause-workplace-toolkit-trade-unionists-wales-tuc-cymru [Accessed 17 November 2022].

Women and Equalities Committee (WEC) (2022) *Menopause and the Workplace*, [online] 28 July. Available from: https://committees.parliament.uk/work/1416/menopause-and-the-workplace/ [Accessed 17 November 2022].

Yoeli, H., Macnaughton, J. and McLusky, S. (2021) 'Menopausal symptoms and work: A narrative review of women's experiences in casual, informal, or precarious jobs', *Maturitas*, 150(August): 14–21.

2

Bodies of Change: Menopause as Biopsychosocial Process

Karen Throsby and Celia Roberts

Introduction

It is a little-known fact that only humans and two species of whale go through menopause. We learned this during a 2016 BBC documentary – 'The whale menopause' – that described menopause as 'one of human evolution's great mysteries' (BBC Radio 4, 2016). Presenting the case of 100+ year-old killer whale ('J2'), anthropomorphically dubbed 'Granny', the programme marvelled at the centrality of the non-reproductive female to the survival of the family group, or pod, concluding that older female killer whales are 'not redundant. They actually have an important role to play'. Granny's physical capacity to 'prolifically' breach (that is, to rise out of the water) was also noted as marvellous, given her age. In 2017, when her death was announced, Granny was described as 'the leader' and 'matriarch' of the group in a BBC radio report (BBC Radio 4, 2017). The interviewed scientist stated that 'post-reproductive females' like Granny direct the pod to navigate safely through foraging grounds, 'storing ecological knowledge for the group'. Dependent adult sons (age 30+ years) are, the scientist reported, eight times more likely to perish when post-reproductive females die: these sons are dependent on their mothers for food. Again, it was confirmed that the females of only two species of whale and humans live beyond their reproductive years.

Humans, the 2016 documentary explained, have much to learn from this fact in understanding the value of older women's lives. It suggested that the story of the killer whales has the empowering potential for appreciating 'the importance of older females in society' (BBC Radio 4, 2016). For us, this conclusion indicates the astonishing depth and strength of prevailing accounts of women's core value as reproductive beings and of menopause as a catastrophic ending to reproductive capacities. Although extensively studied within biology and medicine, menopause remains 'a mystery' because of the persistent social, cultural and scientific difficulties in conceptualizing female human and non-human animals' value beyond species propagation. For example, one attempt to explain human (and whale) menopause is the 'grandmother hypothesis', which posits that post-reproductive life enables females to invest in their own offspring's offspring in order to secure their own genetic survival. Menopause in this context has variously been discussed as an adaptation to allow for this investment or as a byproduct of longevity that has enabled such investment (Peccei, 2001). Either way, the frame of reference remains determinedly reproductive and female longevity beyond the reproductive years always demands explanation. As feminist anthropologist Margaret Lock argued in 1993,

> Women have a better survival rate than men, this cannot be denied, but the very fact that they live longer seems to count against them. Elderly women can only be troublesome to society, it seems, as though the present average life expectancy for men is the way things should be and anything more is unnecessary, especially if these women can contribute neither to the continuity of the species nor to the pleasure of men. (Lock, 1993, pp 365–66)

Biomedical definitions of menopause carry the freight of these longstanding cultural difficulties, typically articulating menopause as an 'end' of something 'reproductive' and 'natural'. The 2015 National Institute for Health and Care Excellence (NICE) Guidance, for example, defines menopause as 'when a woman stops having periods as she reaches the end of her natural reproductive life' (NICE, 2015, p 24).[1] The use of the cessation of menstruation here as the defining point of change creates a firm break in fertility that fails to reflect women's experiences of declining fertility over a decade or more prior to menopause itself – something that women who have not reproduced find themselves constantly reminded of as they progress through their 30s and into their 40s (Faux, 1984; Monach, 1993; Morell, 1994; Tyler May, 1995; Throsby, 2004). In this sense, menopause is the final nail in a very long coffin and, regardless of *when* menopause is deemed to have taken place, its dominant framing is mired in the rhetorics of momentous failure and loss.

According to the British Menopause Society (BMS), for instance, menopause is 'a major life event affecting all women, in a variety of ways, both short and long term' (Currie, Abernethy and Hamoda, 2020, p 1). Furthermore, for both NICE and the BMS, as well as in everyday working and social life, menopause is strongly associated with a raft of unpleasant physical effects, long-term health risks and physical vulnerabilities, including: 'hot flushes and sweats, tiredness and sleep disturbance, joint and muscle ache, heart palpitations, mood swings, anxiety and depression, forgetfulness, lack of concentration, vaginal dryness, vulval irritation, discomfort during sex, loss of interest in sex and increased urinary frequency or urgency'. This, the BMS warn the reader, 'is not an exhaustive list' (Currie, Abernethy and Hamoda, 2020: 3). Such symptoms should, they argue, typically be treated by hormone replacement therapy (HRT) as well as 'lifestyle' interventions like weight loss, smoking cessation, reduced alcohol consumption and increased exercise (Currie, Abernethy and Hamoda, 2020, pp 4–5).

This chapter argues that this dominant framing of menopause as defined by loss and failure not only limits the questions that can be asked about menopausal experience but also the solutions that can be imagined for the challenges that menopause poses both within and beyond the world of work. As suggested in endnote 1, it also limits the kinds of people considered to experience menopause to those who live as their at-birth assigned sex, failing to pay attention to people who have undergone gender transition or who are not clearly male or female physiologically. In making this argument, we are not denying the challenges that menopausal experiences can pose. Nor do we wish to debate the rights and wrongs of controversial interventions such as hormone replacement therapies. Instead, we want to experiment with conceptualizing the menopause not as an ending but as a transition – a biopsychosoocial process (Roberts, 2015) enacted through a range of practices, emotions and effects, which is characterized not by a categorical break in the continuity of women's lives through the collapse of order into disorder, or from fecundity to barrenness, but rather 'as moves from one kind of order to another' (Komesaroff, Rothfield and Daly, 1997, p 5); embodied but not necessarily binarily sexed moves that may be experienced as positive, at least some of the time. In this way, we argue for the opening up of questions foreclosed by the dominant framing of deficit; questions that will allow us to search for more interesting, creative and inclusive answers.

To develop this argument, we begin by outlining the ways in which contemporary framings of menopause appear self-evident but are contingent on historical framings of sex/gender/reproduction and histories of endocrinological knowledge. We then demonstrate how contemporary menopause research has been shaped by these assumptions. We do this, first, by highlighting the ways in which an emphasis on women as ignorant about menopause ignores the location of contemporary menopause within what Wilmut, Campbell and Tudge (2000) call the 'age of biological control'; and, second, by discussing how the dominant historical framing of menopause has led to a research focus on cohorts of white heterosexual cisgendered women with teenage or adult children. As we have already suggested, this excludes, among others: trans and gender diverse people and those with atypical sex; people who have never given birth (either by choice or circumstance); people with disabilities; those going through a premature or medical menopause; and those who become parents later in life, further narrowing an already narrow frame within which menopause can be interrogated and reimagined. If we want to understand the impacts of menopause both within and outside of the workplace, we argue, we need to widen the research frame and ask new questions about menopause as a mid-life, generative process. Indeed, it is only through a more nuanced biopsychosocial framing of the menopause that we can begin to understand its multiple impacts on the complex worlds of work.

Biomedical framings of menopause

A number of feminist researchers have explored the history of menopause as a biomedical and scientific concept. Emerging from early twentieth century European endocrinological science that (re)articulated sex as binary in the face of new findings that sex hormones do not exclusively 'belong' to males or females (Oudshoorn, 1994), physiological changes associated with female ageing were in the 1950s medically reframed in terms of hormonal loss and deficit (Roberts, 2007). From the 1960s onward, female menopause came to be understood as the pathological degeneration of key elements of sexual difference and femininity, including (assumed heterosexual) desire, which were said to depend on oestrogen. Building on the successful chemical isolation of oestrogen in 1929 and the growing capacity to produce pharmaceutical oestrogen-based products from the 1940s onwards, hormonal 'replacement' therapies for menopausal women became widely available in the 1960s and 1970s in the United Kingdom, elsewhere in Europe, North America and Australia. Women were encouraged, through news media, popular books and clinical practices, to view the hormonal processes of ageing through a lens of disease and to seek treatment that would return their bodies to a younger hormonal state (Foxcroft, 2011). A similar framing of male ageing as loss of masculinity did not lead to an equivalent flourishing of testosterone replacement therapies, for complex reasons relating to the availability of research materials, the organization of health care, and cultural framings of sex/gender and age (Marshall, 2007; Roberts, 2007). Female reproductive capacity, of course, cannot be 'replaced' in any straightforward way, as it depends on eggs and ovarian function, as well as sex hormones. Many of the physiological signs of reproductive capacity, however – firm skin, constant temperature, sexual desire, vaginal lubrication, even menstruation – can be affected by exogenous hormones, as in HRT.

In early popular texts, male authors described menopausal bodies with revulsion. Taking hormones was described by North American HRT guru Robert A. Wilson, for example, as curing 'menopausal castration [that] amounts to a mutilation of the whole body' (Wilson, 1966, p 39). Over the last six decades, the language associated with the menopause has changed enormously. It is now less acceptable to write misogynist texts in the name of providing information about women's health. Women have also written personal and analytic accounts of menopause, which, while still typically remaining within the 'end of reproductive life'/'loss of sex hormones' model, are more likely to find some positives in female ageing and menopausal transition (Somers, 2014; Raynor and Fitzgerald, 2018; McLean, 2018; Steinke, 2019). They are also more likely to be more cautious in their approach to HRT, especially since the publication in 2002 of the first Women's Health Initiative Randomized Controlled Trial report, which recorded findings suggesting increased risks of breast cancer and cardiovascular disease (Writing Group for the Women's Health Initiative Randomized Controlled Trial, 2002). These results were later re-evaluated and a recommendation for use with those close to menopause was reinstated (BMS, 2012), but it remains a point of caution for many, as evidenced by the proliferating genre of menopause 'self-help' texts oriented towards achieving a 'natural' menopause. Despite these more positive articulations of menopausal possibility, menopause is still typically figured in terms of health decline and increasing risk of serious illness such as heart disease, osteoporosis and strokes. Little is said, for example, of the ways in which endometriosis sufferers, who constitute approximately 200 million women of reproductive age worldwide (Simmen et al, 2019), experience reprieve at menopause[2] or that some women may experience loss of fertility as a liberation from menstruation, contraception, abortion or unwanted pregnancies (Dillaway, 2005; Ussher, Hawkey and Perz, 2019).

The biomedical framing of menopause as loss also has profound implications for biomedical research and practice. In an editorial comment on the 2015 NICE Guidelines, published in the *British Medical Journal*, biomedical researchers Martha Hickey and Emily Banks (2016) argue that the guidelines pay insufficient attention to treatments or solutions other than HRT, including anti-depressants, yoga and cognitive behavioural therapy (see also Banks, 2015). They are critical of the conclusions drawn about the safety of HRT over the long term, and argue that women should be more fully warned about the risks involved in taking it. Discussing the research agenda laid out in the document, they write,

> It was refreshing to see a research agenda for menopause but disappointing that four out of five items focused on MHT [menopausal hormone therapies]. There are cavernous gaps in the science of menopause: What regulates menopause timing? What is the mechanism of vasomotor symptoms? What causes sleep and mood disturbance? The research agenda is optimistic that further studies of new MHT formulations will show they have greater safety. Given the number of large and costly trials already completed, the justification for further studies seems uncertain and a broader research agenda would be welcome. (Hickey and Banks, 2016, p 1)

Most importantly to us, Hickey and Banks imply that these limited formulations of treatment and research derive from the fact that 'Society has strong negative perceptions of female ageing' (2016, p 2). In line with our argument here, they conclude that 'Wider acceptance that menopause is a normal transition rather than an "oestrogen deficiency syndrome" might be more empowering for women' (2016, p 2) and may even lead to more interesting research questions. We would add that such a reframing might also be empowering for people who do not identify as women. This is not to disregard the hard-to-manage symptoms of menopause that many experience but, rather, to resist the binary of catastrophe or feminine triumph in search of what Dina Giorgis (2013), writing about colonial stories and racial suffering, calls 'the better story' – that is, not a story that occupies a higher place in a moral or cultural hierarchy, but rather one that can capture, even if only provisionally, what is possible beyond a deficit model.

Information deficit models: menopause as an experience of ignorance

Both popular books on menopause and educational materials for clinicians, such as those produced by the British and Australasian Menopause Societies, emphasize the need to educate women about hormonal changes associated with mid-life. The content of such materials is remarkably repetitive and formulaic, while the education itself is consistently figured as rational, factual and impartial. Building on Roberts (2007), we want to suggest that such education schools women (and their partners) in a rather narrow biomedical understanding of ageing, sex/gender, sexuality and reproduction that focuses on negative experiences, and, as mentioned earlier, ignores people who may not identify as cisgendered women. More practically, it is also important to note that, in these texts, women are encouraged to talk to clinicians, which inevitably brings them closer to prescribed pharmaceutical 'solutions' to physical and psychosocial problems (Guillemin, 2000a, 2000b; Roberts and Waldby, 2021), while those who are not 'women' are left to find their own solutions.

Despite the proliferation of these texts, the British Menopause Society (2016), responding to the launch of the 2015 NICE guidelines, declared that too many women – up to 50 per cent – are ill advisedly choosing to 'suffer in silence' rather than seek medical help, later arguing that 'incorrect interpretation of data and sensational media reporting' has led to 'non-informed decision-making' in relation to HRT (Currie, Abernethy and Hamoda, 2020, p 4). Women experiencing menopause are figured as poorly informed and thus at risk not only of physical and mental health problems but also of declining productivity in both the private and public domains. In 2015, then Chief Medical Officer, Professor Dame Sally Davies, recommended that workplaces become more 'menopause aware' in order to protect the necessary productivity of middle-aged women (Department of Health, 2015). Chapters in this volume address this issue in depth.

Within the contemporary biomedical model of menopause, then, information deficit accounts for women's failure to attend medical clinics to discuss menopause, to comply with clinical advice or to conform to mainstream narratives of menopausal experience as loss and suffering. This framing reflects wider assumptions of counter-normative health behaviours as evidence of knowledge deficit, which can be rectified through information dissemination (for example, in the case of 'lifestyle' health information campaigns around obesity, smoking or alcohol consumption). The assumption here is that, once people know, they will do the 'right thing', rendering refusals to do so deviant and pathological. The inadequacy of this approach is evident in the relentless flood of information aimed at facilitating weight loss, which the targets of those information flows can reproduce easily when prompted even while resisting it, or deprioritizing it, in everyday life (Thompson and Kumar, 2011; Cappellini, Harmna and Parsons, 2018). Indeed, refusals of received menopausal 'truths' (or other health advice) are themselves figured as a form of 'suffering'; the possibility that they could be expressions of positive desire, or the result of informed choice, is not countenanced. As Paula Treichler observed in relation to public health communications around AIDS:

> [we] do not passively receive and internalise definitions and facts provided by authorities, rather, we talk about them with our friends, argue about how to interpret them, think about how they will apply to our everyday lives and work out what is gained or lost by adopting new behaviour and what that implies about our identity. (1999, p 267)

This figuration of menopausal women as ignorant sits incongruously alongside the fact that the current mid-life generation of assigned-female-at-birth (AFAB) people have encountered a lifetime of hormonal and technological interventions into the reproductive body, including the contraceptive pill and fertility treatments – either directly through use or, at least, through awareness (and perhaps repudiation) of those interventions. It is hard to conceive of them as likely to be ignorant of hormonal processes and medications. Of course, those who identify as trans or gender-fluid or those who have been diagnosed as having atypical sexual development may well also have such expertise. This generation of AFAB women has also experienced two decades of online health information – as Sally Wyatt et al (2005) have discussed in relation to the menopause transition – as well as the widespread effects of feminist health movements advocating women's education and proactive relationship to their bodies and health (Boston Women's Health Book Collective, 1989; Smith, 1995; Morgen, 2002; Ehrenreich and English, 2005; Davis, 2007; Murphy, 2012). Ussher, Hawkey and Perz (2019), for example, found a strong effect of feminist health discourses on many women in their study of Australian and Canadian migrants' experiences of menopause: they analyse this effect in terms of the emergence of a resistance to negative biomedical models.

Thinking even more broadly, we note that the contemporary menopausal generation are living in 'the age of biological control' (Wilmut, Campbell and Tudge, 2000). This marks a time in which citizens (particularly women) are expected to actively pursue their health through engaging with medical and scientific knowledge, pharmaceutical products and digital technologies that track and monitor the body (Lupton, 2016; Mort et al, 2016; Roberts and Waldby, 2021). And while those expectations and practices are firmly, and problematically, located within a relentlessly middle-class milieu, the figuration of women as ignorantly suffering in silence sits at odds with evidence that health consumers are increasingly proactive in tracking, managing and researching physical processes and experiences. As such, the premise that 'if only women knew …' falls far short of being able to account for menopausal experience and meaning, both in its own terms and in the fields of inquiry that it forecloses.

Feminist articulations of menopause

There is a long and vociferous radical feminist history of resistance towards biomedical intervention into bodies coded as female, with new reproductive technologies, for example, conceptualized as patriarchal efforts to contain and control women's bodies to maintain the asymmetrical gender order and protect the interests of capital (Spallone and Steinberg, 1987; Rowland, 1992; Raymond, 1993). In relation to menopause transitions, HRT has been the primary target of this politicized refusal, with scholars and popular writers criticizing the experimental nature of these medications, the investment of the pharmaceutical industry in profit over women's well-being, and the repudiation of women's 'natural' ageing processes (Greer, 1993; Coney, 1995; Coupland and Williams, 2002; Foxcroft, 2011). Passionately invested in women's well-being, this approach is typically reliant on a 'natural' female body that is disarticulated from the complex social worlds in which bodies come into being and are lived. Furthermore, such arguments trap conceptualizations of menopause in entrenched debates around HRT that inescapably narrow the field of vision and delimit the questions that can be asked (see also Ballard et al, 2009; Dillaway and Burton, 2011).

Our approach learns from this history of resistance, but takes a different path, articulating menopausal bodies as biopsychosocial. The extensive feminist literature on the body and its processes as inseparable from the world and from any individual's life experience, we argue, offers a way out of constraining 'for or against' arguments about HRT and the nature of menopausal bodies. This literature includes, for example, research articulating new reproductive technologies as processes rather than technical procedures (Throsby, 2004; Wilson, 2006); refiguring the hormonal body (Yancey, Ortega and Kumanyika, 2006; Roberts, 2007, 2015); rethinking menopause as a locally particular rather than universal phenomenon (Lock, 1993; Atkinson et al, 2021); exploring metaphors for making sense of menopause transitions (Martin, 1997); and articulating genealogies that highlight the inextricability of menopause transitions from the wider social context within which they are experienced (Sybylla, 1997; Houck, 2006).

Bodies that count

One of the striking features of research on menopause, particularly within the social sciences, is a reliance on easier-to-access homogenous cohorts of middle-class, cisgendered, heterosexual women (for example, de Salis et al, 2018). Many studies focus on white women, although a growing literature on menopause experiences among ethnic minorities is beginning to address this issue (for example Agee, 2000; Wray, 2007; Dillaway et al, 2008; Murphy et al, 2016; Sievert et al, 2016; Ussher, Hawkey and Perz, 2019). Prevailing public and biomedical framings exclude the experiences and desires of many whose lives do not fit conventional reproductive and hormonal patterns, or who occupy disadvantaged social positions. This includes those whose opportunities for information, choice and control in relation to health, and particularly reproduction, have been actively constrained – for example, women with learning and physical disabilities and those from economically disadvantaged situations (Feinberg, 2001; Graham, 2009; Emerson and Baines, 2011). Looking beyond an additive approach whereby new cohorts are folded into existing conceptual frameworks, a biopsychosocial approach demands consideration of how concerns about reproductive and physical changes intersect with other responses to, experiences of, and contexts surrounding menopause. This includes not only those most intensely subject to social expectations of self-care and bodily discipline – for example, women experiencing involuntary childlessness (Throsby, 2004) – but also those whose opportunities for information, choice and control are limited, or whose bodies are less likely to be conceptualized (either by themselves or by others) in reproductive terms.

A non-exhaustive selection of those whose menopausal experiences are typically overlooked in medical and social research includes LGBTQI+ people, those with disabilities, people undergoing a premature menopause and those who have never given birth, either by choice or circumstance (Atkinson et al, 2021). In the case of LGBTQI+ people, for example, the limited menopause research focuses on the social risks and possibilities of the menopause among lesbians (Hyde et al, 2011) or on sex post-menopause, usually in comparison to heterosexual experiences (Winterich, 2003, 2007). An exception here is Kelly's (2005) interview-based study of lesbian menopausal experience, which actively resists this comparative impulse, insisting on centralizing lesbian experience and looking beyond the biological to include the psychosocial. Menopause is similarly absent from the trans literature, except for the use of HRT as a point of reference for discussions of hormone use, and there is scant research on the implications of ageing for trans-related hormonal regimens (although for exceptions see Mohamed and Hunter, 2014; Siverskog, 2015).

There is also a paucity of work on the experiences and understandings of menopause transitions among those with disabilities, where both research and services have concentrated on puberty, menstruation and sexual activity (Martin et al, 2003; Fish, 2016a, 2016b), or, more biomedically, on the timing of menopause (for example, Schupf et al, 1997). In 1995, Carr and Hollins reported the absence of any significant body of knowledge about experiences of menopause among those with learning disabilities and, in 2008, Willis noted how little the body of work had expanded since then. Existing research highlights the need for accessible information sources for those experiencing menopause, support for those caring for them and the importance of opportunities to consider positive aspects of menopausal transitions (Martin et al, 2003; McCarthy, 2002; McCarthy and Millard, 2003). More recent research on the experiences of menopause among autistic people highlights a similar paucity of appropriate information and support, as well as the challenges of managing both new and pre-existing social, emotional, cognitive and sensory difficulties which can be exacerbated by the onset of menopause (Moseley, Druce, and Turner-Cobb, 2020; Karavidas and de Visser, 2021). Research on physical disabilities and menopause also addresses the potential exacerbation of existing conditions (Vandenakker and Glass, 2001); potential barriers to accessing screening programmes (Weiner, Simon and Weiner, 2002); the importance of healthcare providers' recommendations in decision-making, particularly in relation to HRT (Becker, Stuifenbergen and Gordon, 2002); the need for information and guidance addressing the particular needs and desires of disabled people (Dormire and Becker, 2007; Harrison and Becker, 2007); and the importance of not focusing on menopause to the exclusion of the wider social context and its accompanying stressors for those with disabilities (Kalpakjian and Leqeurica, 2006). Each of these small pockets of publication emphasize the urgent need for more research into these largely excluded experiences.

Both premature menopause and the experiences of those going through menopause who have never given birth have received more attention in the literature, albeit in constrained ways. 'Premature menopause' is used to describe those entering the menopause before the age of 40 (Torrealday and Pal, 2015). It can occur spontaneously or be induced, related to autoimmune syndromes, genetic conditions (such as Turner Syndrome), ovarian toxins (chemotherapy, radiation) or surgery. It affects around 1 per cent of women and is understood as having a 'high symptom and quality-of-life burden including menopausal, sexual and cognitive symptoms as well as infertility' (Moore et al, 2019, p 210). The literature highlights the common experience of spontaneous premature menopause going unrecognized in clinical consultations (Milsom and O'Sullivan, 2017; Conway, 2019), leaving those experiencing symptoms feeling isolated and uninformed, while for cancer patients, concerns around menopause (and fertility loss) exist alongside, and sometimes in tension with, the pressing demands of cancer treatment (Porroche-Escudero, 2016; Parton, Ussher and Perz, 2017). Much of the available medical literature also focuses on improved care practices: in an article on best nursing practices, Conway (2019, p 803) concludes that there is a need to 'adapt the level of information and types of treatment according to life circumstances', proposing the adaptation must be informed by a thorough evidence base of women's experiences. In relation to those who have never given birth, either by choice or circumstance, the limited research focuses on menopause as either a tragic finality to thwarted efforts to give birth to a baby (Friese et al, 2006; Ferland and Caron, 2013); a controversial site of New Reproductive Technologies (NRT)-assisted reproduction among older women (Bahn et al, 2010); or a release from the threat of either unwanted pregnancy or the stresses of infertility (Olshansky, 2005). This reproductive lens, we suggest, obscures other biopsychosocial dimensions of menopausal transitions, delimiting the questions that can be asked and the solutions that can be imagined, both within and outside of work.

The case for the inclusion of under-represented cohorts in scientific and social scientific research is based not simply on filling 'gaps', but rather, following bell hooks (1984), moves excluded experiences from margin to centre to prompt a re-imagining of the social and research field. This enables us not simply to ask about what is missing from our prevailing understandings of menopause as lacunae to be filled, but rather to interrogate why and how non-normative perspectives are so easily overlooked and what difference it makes to public, personal and clinical responses to menopause when diverse relationships with the technologies of reproduction and hormonal intervention (and therefore with menopause itself) are placed at the centre of inquiry. For example, by focusing on cohorts who are largely unaccounted for in mainstream policy and practice, we can ask new questions critical to contemporary lives: What does a framing of menopause as the end of fertility mean to someone who is in/voluntarily childless? What do trans people do with their hormonal regimes around menopause? How does menopause as part of cancer treatment or gender transition challenge us to rethink gendered narratives of menopausal transitions and (healthy) ageing? How do those identifying as LGBTQI+ feel about menopausal hormonal changes widely decried as problematic because they are 'de-gendering' (such as increased facial hair)?

'There is no such thing as *the* menopause'

Central to this expanded biopsychosocial understanding, and the questions that it opens up, is the realization that 'there is no such thing as *the* menopause' (Komesaroff, Rothfield and Daly, 1997, p 13). As Melby, Lock and Kaufert (2005, p 507) also conclude, '[there] is no universal menopausal entity or experience waiting to be exposed through systematic inquiry'. As such, the goal of any research or intervention in this field should aim to highlight specificities and differences, rather than to uncover foundational commonalities inherent to a singularly knowable physiological process. The menopause is not *the* Change, as it is ominously known, but a shifting constellation of biopsychosocial changes (Hunter and Edozien, 2017), with bodies conceptualized not only as *changing* but also as subject to *being changed* (for example as a result of surgical, radiotherapeutic or hormonal intervention) and as *enacting change* in environment and social relations (such as in the workplace – see for example Hardy, Griffiths and Hunter, 2017; Jack, Riach and Bariola, 2019), both reflecting and producing transformations in the employment patterns, caring responsibilities and visibility of mid-life and older women in public life. As such, these attempted re-imaginings of menopause should not hold the biomedical model in place and add layers of nuance and diversity on top but rather speak to the need to reimagine the medical model itself, as Hickey and Banks (2016) suggest earlier.

This proposed shift away from a strictly biomedical imaginary of menopause towards a biopsychosocial lens that keeps a greater diversity of experience in view aligns with recent biomedical, social scientific and policy arguments for better understandings of menopause. For example, Brewis et al (2017, p 15) observed in their evidence review of the effects of menopause on women's economic participation that there is a serious lack of knowledge about the ways in which employers and the government could better support those experiencing menopausal transitions. Indeed, it is important to note that those in the overlooked cohorts we have described earlier also perform both paid and unpaid work, and their experiences speak directly not only to menopausal experience in the workplace, but also to the wider social and cultural context within which those experiences are navigated and made meaningful. In a similar vein, a 2015 review in *Maturitas* argued for 'a new conceptual framework for a healthy menopause', which will take the physical social and psychological elements of this transition into account (Jaspers et al, 2015), while a 2016 article in the same journal describes the need for a new 'model of care for healthy menopause' (Stute et al, 2016).

These calls for more nuanced accounts of menopause also resonate with burgeoning interest in the popular domain and within policy circles as other chapters in this book describe. While we are pleased to see TV documentaries such as Kirsty Wark's 'The menopause and me' (BBC2, 2017) and Mariella Frostrup's 'The truth about the menopause' (BBC1, 2018), as well as published first-person accounts, we are concerned that, even within these, menopausal transitions are positioned as something to be confessed (McLean, 2018), held at bay (Somers, 2014) or befriended (Raynor and Fitzgerald, 2018). We note, more positively, however, that sometimes authors agree that menopause should be reimagined (Steinke, 2019) or, similarly, as Jack, Riach and Bariola suggest relating to their qualitative interview data, 'The sentiment of going unscripted was often part of a broader story of the menopausal body, in the sense that the ambiguity of menopause provided an experiential site for the unknown' (2019, p 137). While this flourishing interest clearly signals an unmet demand for expanded and nuanced re-imaginings of an experience that is at once shared and unique, known and unrecognizable, it is important to keep an eye on whose voices and experiences get airplay.

Conclusion

We started this chapter with whales not just as an interesting hook, but to pose questions about how far we might push current thinking about menopause. 'Granny' the whale was smart, resourceful and central to the survival of her pod. She did not appear to be suffering from hormone-related decline or mourning the loss of her reproductive function (although how could we know?). For us, she is an inspiration in many regards. The perplexity she triggers, however, also points to hugely restrictive modes of thought that continue to shape scientific, biomedical and cultural thinking about ageing bodies, sexuality and sex/gender. We have argued in this chapter that existing research tends to repeat well-worn stories of loss and decline, (re)producing menopause as something to be dreaded and treated, and framing those who refuse treatment as woefully ignorant. It is time to break out of this circular trap, to listen more carefully to people's experiences and to create new stories.

Notes

1   Here, as in most literature on the menopause, the word 'women' is used to designate those undergoing 'female menopause'. Some scientists and clinicians also talk about 'male menopause', an ageing-related set of hormonal changes in people with male physiology and assigned male at birth. As we discuss, menopause-related changes also occur in trans, gender-fluid and gender-queer people and people of atypical sexual differentiation, but may have unique characteristics connected to individuals' histories of taking exogenous hormones and/or endogenous hormonal differences. There is very little research on these experiences. In this text we use the word 'women' when referring to specific knowledge and arguments about cisgendered people assigned female at birth, fully acknowledging that there are also other kinds of women who may have different experiences of ageing and that some men and others who do not identify as men or women may also experience related kinds of issues because they have elements of 'female' physiology.

2   The webpage of the Australasian Menopause Society reports that there is 'sparse' evidence about the safety and efficacy of HRT for people with endometriosis. See https://www.menopause.org.au/hp/information-sheets/1401-endometriosis-management-after-menopause.

References

Agee, E. (2000) 'Menopause and the transition of women's knowledge: African American and white women's perspectives', *Medical Anthropology Quarterly*, 14(1): 73–93.

Atkinson, C., Beck, V., Brewis, J., Davies, A. and Duberley, J. (2021) 'Menopause and the workplace: New directions in HRM research and HR practice', *Human Resource Management Journal*, 31(1): 49–64.

Bahn, D., Havemann, D.L. and Phelps, J.Y. (2010) 'Reproduction beyond the menopause: How old is too old for assisted reproductive technology?', *Journal of Assisted Reproduction and Genetics*, 27(7): 365–70.

Ballard, K.D., Elston, M.A. and Gave, J. (2009) 'Private and public ageing in the UK: The transition through menopause', *Current Sociology*, 57(2): 269–90.

Banks, E. (2015) 'An evidence-based future for menopausal hormone therapy', *Women's Health*, 11(6): 785–8.

BBC1 (2018) 'The truth about the menopause', 26 November.

BBC2 (2017) 'Kirsty Wark: the menopause and me', BBC 2, 8 August.

BBC Radio 4 (2016) 'The whale menopause', [online] 18 February, Available from: https://www.bbc.co.uk/programmes/b07mxv62#:~:text=The%20females%20of%20both%20species,another%20species%20of%20toothed%20whale [Accessed 4 April 2022].

BBC Radio 4 (2017) 'Inside Science: RIP Granny the oldest orca', [online] 5 January, Available from: https://www.bbc.co.uk/programmes/b086kxwy [Accessed 4 April 2022].

Becker, H., Stuifenbergen, A.K. and Gordon, D. (2002) 'The decision to take hormone replacement therapy among women with disabilities', *Western Journal of Nursing Research*, 24(3): 264–81.

Boston Women's Health Book Collective (1989) *The New Our Bodies, Ourselves: A Health Book by and for Women*, London: Penguin.

Brewis, J., Beck, V., Davies, A. and Matheson, J. (2017) *The Impact of Menopause Transition on Women's Economic Participation in the UK*, [online] 20 July, Available from: https://www.gov.uk/government/publications/ menopause-transition-effects-on-womens-economic-participation [Accessed 17 November 2022].

British Menopause Society (2016) 'The Women's Health Initiative Study and hormone therapy – what have we learned 10 years on?', [online] 22 May, Available from: https://thebms.org.uk/2012/05/the-womens-health-initiative-study-and-hormone-therapy-what-have-we-learned-10-years-on/ [Accessed 4 April 2022].

Cappellini, B., Harmna, V. and Parsons, E. (2018) 'Unpacking the lunchboxes: Biopedagogies, mothering and social class', *Sociology of Health and Illness*, 40(7): 1200–14.

Carr, J. and Hollins, S. (1995) 'Menopause in women with learning disabilities', *Journal of Intellectual Disability Research*, 39(2): 137–39.

Coney, S. (1995) *The Menopause Industry: How the Medical Establishment Exploits Women*, London: Women's Press.

Conway, G.S. (2019) 'Premature ovarian insufficiency, menopause and hormone replacement therapy', in Llahana, S., Follin, C., Yedinak, C. and Grossman, A. (eds) *Advanced Practice in Endocrinology Nursing*, Chamonix: Springer, pp 803–15.

Coupland, J. and Williams, A. (2002) 'Conflicting discourses, shifting ideologies: Pharmaceutical, "alternative" and feminist emancipatory texts on the menopause', *Discourse & Society*, 13(4): 419–45.

Currie, H., Abernethy, K. and Hamoda, H. (2020) *Vision for Menopause Care in the UK*, London: British Menopause Society.

Davis, K. (2007) *The Making of Our Bodies, Ourselves: How Feminism Travels Across Borders*, Durham, NC: Duke University Press.

Department of Health (2015) Annual Report of the Chief Medical Officer, 2014. The Health of the 51%: Women [online] 11 December, Available from: https://www.gov.uk/government/publications/chief-medical-officer-annual-report-2014-womens-health [Accessed 26 July 2023].

De Salis, I., Owen-Smith, A., Donovan, J.L. and Lawlor, D.A. (2018) 'Experiencing menopause in the UK: The interrelated narratives of normality, distress and transformation', *Journal of Women and Aging*, 30(6): 520–40.

Dillaway, H.E. (2005) 'Menopause is the "good old": Women's thoughts about reproductive agency', *Gender & Society*, 19(3): 398–417.

Dillaway, H.E. and Burton, J. (2011) '"Not done yet?!" Women discuss the "end" of menopause', *Women's Studies*, 40(2): 149–76.

Dillaway, H.E., Byrnes, M., Miller, S. and Rehan, S. (2008) 'Talking "among us": How women from different racial-ethnic groups define and discuss the menopause', *Health Care for Women International*, 29(7): 766–81.

Dormire, S. and Becker, H. (2007) 'Menopause health decision support for women with physical disabilities', *Journal of Obstetric, Gynecologic and Neonatal Nursing*, 36(1): 97–104.

Ehrenreich, B. and English, D. (2005) *For Her Own Good: Two Centuries of the Experts' Advice to Women*, New York: Anchor Books.

Emerson, E. and Baines, S. (2011) 'Health inequalities and people with learning disabilities in the UK', *Tizard Learning Disabilities Review*, 16(1): 42–8.

Faux, M. (1984) *Childless by Choice: Choosing Childlessness in the Eighties*, New York, Garden City, NY: Anchor Press/Doubleday.

Feinberg, L. (2001) 'Trans health crisis: For us it's life or death', *American Journal of Public Health*, 91(6): 897–900.

Ferland, P. and Caron, S.L. (2013) 'Exploring the long-term impact of female infertility: A qualitative analysis of interviews with postmenopausal women who remained childless', *The Family Journal: Counselling and Therapy for Couples and Families*, 21(2): 180–8.

Fish, R.M. (2016a) 'Friends and family: Regulation and relationships on the locked ward', *Disability and Society*, 31(10): 1385–1402.

Fish, R.M. (2016b) '"They've said I'm vulnerable with men": Doing sexuality on locked wards', *Sexualities*, 19(5–6): 641–58.

Foxcroft, N. (2011) *Hot Flushes, Cold Science: A History of the Modern Menopause*, London: Granta.

Friese, C., Becker, G. and Nachtigall, R.D. (2006) 'Rethinking the biological clock: Eleventh hour moms, miracle moms and the meanings of age-related fertility', *Social Science and Medicine*, 63(6): 1550–60.

Georgis, D. (2013) *The Better Story: Queer Affects from the Middle East*, New York: SUNY Press.

Graham, H. (ed) (2009) *Understanding Health Inequalities*, Milton Keynes: Open University Press.

Greer, G. (1993) *The Change: Women, Aging and the Menopause*, New York: Ballantine.

Guillemin, M. (2000a) 'Blood, bone, women and HRT: Co-construction in the menopause clinic', *Australian Feminist Studies*, 15(32): 191–203.

Guilllemin, M. (2000b) 'Working practices of the menopause clinic', *Science, Technology and Human Values*, 25(4): 448–70.

Hardy, C., Griffiths, A. and Hunter, M.S. (2017) 'What do working women want? A qualitative investigation into women's perspectives on employer and line manager support', *Maturitas*, 101: 37–41.

Harrison, T. and Becker, H. (2007) 'A qualitative study of menopause among women with disabilities', *Advances in Nursing Science*, 30(2): 123–38.

Hickey, M. and Banks, E. (2016) 'NICE guidelines on the menopause', *British Medical Journal*, 352(191): i191.

hooks, b. (1984) *Feminist Theory: From Margin to Centre*, Boston, MA: South End Press.

Houck, J.A. (2006) *Hot and Bothered: Women, Medicine and Menopause in Modern America*, Cambridge, MA: Harvard University Press.

Hunter, M.S. and Edozien, L.C. (2017) 'Special issue on biopsychosocial perspectives on the menopause', *Journal of Psychosomatic Obstetrics and Gynaecology*, 38(3): 159–60.

Hyde, A., Nee, J., Howlett, E., Butler, M. and Drennan, J. (2011) 'The ending of menstruation: Perspectives and experiences of lesbian and heterosexual women', *Journal of Women and Aging*, 23(2): 160–76.

Jack, G., Riach, K. and Bariola, E. (2019) 'Temporality and gendered agency: Menopausal subjectivities in women's work', *Human Relations*, 72(1): 122–43.

Jaspers, L., Dean, N.M.P., van Dijk, G.M., Muka, T., Wen, K., Meun, C. et al (2015) 'Health in middle aged and elderly women: A conceptual framework for a healthy menopause', *Maturitas*, 81(1): 93–8.

Kalpakjian, C.Z. and Lequerica, A. (2006) 'Quality of life and menopause in women with physical disabilities', *Journal of Women's Health*, 15(9): 1014–27.

Karavidas, M. and de Visser, R.O. (2021) '"It's not just in my head and it's not irrelevant": Autistic negotiations of menopausal transition', *Journal of Autism Development Disorders*, 52: 1143–55.

Kelly, J. (2005) *Zest for Life: Lesbians' Experiences of the Menopause*, Melbourne: Spinifax Press.

Komesaroff, P., Rothfield, P. and Daly, J. (1997) 'Introduction. Mapping menopause: Objectivity or multiplicity?', in Komesaroff, P., Rothfield, P. and Daly, J. (eds) *Reinterpreting Menopause: Cultural and Philosophical Issues*, London: Routledge, pp 3–16.

Lock, M. (1993) *Encounters with Aging: Mythologies of Menopause in Japan and North America*, London: University of California Press.

Lupton, D. (2016) *The Quantified Self: A Sociology of Self-Tracking*, Cambridge: Polity Press.

Marshall, B.L. (2007) 'Climacteric redux: (Re)medicalising the male menopause', *Men & Masculinities*, 9(4): 509–29.

Martin, E. (1997) 'The woman in the menopausal body', in Komesaroff, P., Rothfield, P. and Daly, J. (eds) *Reinterpreting Menopause: Cultural and Philosophical Issues*, London: Routledge, pp 239–54.

Martin, D., Kakumani, S., Martin, M. and Cassidy, G. (2003) 'Learning disabilities and the menopause', *Post Reproductive Health: The Journal of the British Menopause Society*, 9(1): 22–6.

McCarthy, M. (2002) 'Going through the menopause: Perceptions and experiences of women with intellectual difficulties', *Journal of Intellectual and Developmental Disability*, 27(4): 281–95.

McCarthy, M. and Millard, L. (2003) 'Discussing the menopause with women with learning disabilities', *British Journal of Learning Disabilities*, 31: 9–17.

McLean, A. (2018) *Confessions of a Menopausal Woman*, London: Corgi Books.

Melby, M.K., Lock, M. and Kaufert, P. (2005) 'Culture and symptom reporting at menopause', *Human Reproduction Update*, 11(5): 495–512.

Milsom, S. and O'Sullivan, S. (2017) 'Premature ovarian insufficiency', *O&G Magazine*, 19(1): 29–32.

Mohamed, S. and Hunter, M. (2014) 'Transgender women's experiences and beliefs about hormone therapy through and beyond mid-age', *International Journal of Transgenderism* 20(1): 98–107.

Monach, J.H. (1993) *Childless, No Choice: The Experience of Involuntary Childlessness*, London: Routledge.

Moore, H.C.F., Unger, J.M., Phillips, K-A., Boyle, F., Hitre, E., Moseley, A. et al (2019) 'Final analysis of the Prevention of Early Menopause Study (POEMS)/ SWOG Intergroup S0230', *Journal of the National Cancer Institute*, 111(2): 210–13.

Morell, M.M. (1994) *Unwomanly Conduct: The Challenges of Intentional Childlessness*, London: Routledge.

Morgen, S. (2002) *Into Our Own Hands: The Women's Health Movement in the United States, 1969–1990*, New Brunswick: Rutgers University Press.

Mort, M., Roberts, C., Furbo, M., Wilkinson, J. and Mackenzie, A. (2016) 'Biosensing: How citizens' views illuminate emerging health and social risks', *Health, Risk and Society*, 17(7–8): 605–23.

Moseley, R.L., Druce, T., Turner-Cobb, J.M. (2020) '"When my autism broke": A qualitative study spotlighting autistic voices on menopause', *Autism*, 24(6): 1423–37.

Murphy, M. (2012) *Seizing the Means of Reproduction: Entanglements of Feminism, Health and Technoscience*, Durham, NC: Duke University Press.

Murphy, L., Sievert, L., Begum, K., Sharmeen, T., Puleo, E., Chowdhury et al (2016) 'Life course effects on age at menopause among Bangladeshi sedentees and migrants to the UK', *American Journal of Human Biology*, 25(1): 83–93.

National Institute for Health and Care Excellence (2015) *Menopause: Diagnosis and Management*, London: National Institute for Health and Care Excellence.

Olshansky, E. (2005) 'Feeling normal: Women's experiences of menopause after infertility', *American Journal of Maternal Child Nursing*, 30(3): 195–200.

Oudshoorn, N. (1994) *Beyond the Natural Body: An Archaeology of Sex Hormones*, London: Routledge.

Parton, C., Ussher, J. and Perz, J. (2017) 'Experiencing menopause in the context of cancer: Women's constructions of gendered subjectivities', *Psychology and Health*, 32(9): 1109–26.

Peccei, J. (2001) 'A critique of the grandmother hypothesis: Old and new', *American Journal of Human Biology*, 13(4): 434–52.

Porroche-Escudero, A. (2016) 'Oncofertility: Beyond biological motherhood, towards reproductive justice', *Breast Cancer Consortium Quarterly*, [online] 3, 20 September, Available from: https://breastcancerconsortium.net/oncofertility-beyond-biological-motherhood-towards-reproductive-justice/ [Accessed 4 April 2022].

Raymond, J.G. (1993) *Women as Wombs: Reproductive Technologies and the Battle over Women's Freedom*, San Francisco: Harper San Francisco.

Raynor, S. and Fitzgerald, P. (2018) *Making Friends with the Menopause*, Brighton: Creative Pumpkin.

Roberts, C. (2007) *Messengers of Sex: Hormones, Biomedicine and Feminism*, Cambridge: Cambridge University Press.

Roberts, C. (2015) *Puberty in Crisis: The Sociology of Early Sexual Development*, Cambridge: Cambridge University Press.

Roberts, C. and Waldby, C. (2021) 'Incipient infertility: Tracking eggs and ovulation across the life course', *Catalyst: Feminism, Theory, Technoscience*, 7(1): 1–25.

Rowland, R. (1992) *Living Laboratories: Women and Reproductive Technology*, London: Lime Tree.

Schupf, N., Zigman, W., Kapell, D., Lee, J.H., Kline, J. and Levin, B. (1997) 'Early menopause in women with Down's syndrome', *Journal of Intellectual Disability Research*, 41(3): 264–7.

Sievert, L., Begum, K., Sharmeen, T., Murphy, L., Whitcomb, B.W., Chowdhury, O. et al (2016) 'Hot flash report and measurement among Bangladeshi migrants, their London neighbours and their community of origin', *American Journal of Physical Anthropology*, 161(4): 620–33.

Simmen, R.C.M., Quick, C.M., Kelley, A.S. and Zheng, W. (2019) 'Endometriosis and endometriosis-associated tumors', in Zheng, W., Fadare, O., Quick, C.M., Shen, D., and Guo, D. (eds) *Gynecologic and Obstetric Pathology, Volume 2*, Singapore: Springer Singapore, pp 405–26.

Siverskog, A. (2015) 'Ageing bodies that matter: Age, gender and embodiment in older transgender people's life stories', *NORA – Nordic Journal of Feminist and Gender Research*, 23(1): 4–19.

Smith, S. (1995) *Sick and Tired of Being Sick and Tired*, Philadelphia, PA: University of Pennsylvania Press.

Somers, S. (2014) *I'm Too Young for This: The Natural Hormone Solution to Enjoy Perimenopause*, New York: Harmony Books.

Spallone, P. and Steinberg, D.L (1987) *Made to Order: The Myth of Reproductive and Genetic Progress*, London: Pergamon Press.

Steinke, D (2019) *Flash Count Diary: A New Story About the Menopause*, Edinburgh: Cannongate Books.

Stute, P., Ceausu, I., Depypere, H., Lambrinoudaki, I., Mueck, A., Pérez-López, F.R. et al (2016) 'A model of care for healthy menopause and ageing: EMAS position statement', *Maturitas*, 92(1): 1–6.

Sybylla, R. (1997) 'Situating menopause within the strategies of power: a genealogy', in Komesaroff, P., Rothfield, P. and Daly, J. (eds) *Reinterpreting Menopause: Cultural and Philosophical Issues*, London: Routledge, pp 200–22.

Thompson, L. and Kumar, A. (2011) 'Responses to health promotion campaigns: resistance, denial and othering', *Critical Public Health*, 21(1): 107–17.

Throsby, K. (2004) *When IVF Fails: Feminism, Infertility and the Negotiation of Normality,* Basingstoke: Palgrave.

Torrealday, S. and Pal, L. (2015) 'Premature menopause', *Endocrinology and Metabolism Clinics of North America*, 44(3): 543–57.

Treichler, P.A. (1999) *How to Have a Theory in an Epidemic: Cultural Chronicles of AIDS*, Durham, NC: Duke University Press.

Tyler May, E. (1995) *Barren in the Promised Land: Childless Americans and the Pursuit of Happiness*, Cambridge: Harvard University Press.

Ussher, J., Hawkey, A.J. and Perz, J. (2019) '"Age of despair" or "when life starts": Migrant and refugee women negotiate constructions of menopause', *Culture, Health and Sexuality*, 21(7): 741–56.

Vandenakker, C.B. and Glass, D.D. (2001) 'Menopause and ageing with disability', *Physical Medicine and Rehabilitation Clinics*, 12(1): 133–51.

Weiner, S.L., Simon, J.A. and Weiner, B. (2002) 'Maximising health in menopausal women with disabilities', *Menopause: The Journal of the North American Menopause Society*, 9(3): 208–19.

Willis, D. (2008) 'A decade on: What have we learned about supporting women with intellectual disabilities through the menopause', *Journal of Intellectual Disabilities*, 12(1): 9–23.

Wilmut, I., Campbell, K. and Tudge, C. (2000) *The Second Creation: Dolly and the Age of Biological Control*, London: Headline.

Wilson, R.A. (1966) *Feminine Forever*, New York: M. Evans and Company

Wilson, L.A. (2015) *A Land Mark Walk Reflecting on In/Fertility and Childlessness*, Leeds: Louise Ann Wilson Company Limited.

Winterich, J.A. (2003) 'Sex, menopause and culture: Sexual orientation and the meaning of the menopause for women's sex lives', *Gender and Society*, 17(4): 627–42.

Winterich, J.A. (2007) 'Ageing, femininity and the body: What appearance changes mean to women with age', *Gender Issues*, 24(3): 51–69.

Wray, S. (2007) 'Women making sense of midlife: Ethnic and cultural diversity', *Journal of Aging Studies*, 21(1): 31–45.

Writing Group for the Women's Health Initiative Randomized Controlled Trial (2002) 'Risks and benefits of estrogen plus progestin in healthy post-menopausal women', *Journal of the American Medical Association*, 288(3): 321–3.

Yancey, A., Ortega, A. and Kumanyika, S. (2006) 'Effective recruitment and retention of minority research participants', *Annual Review of Public Health*, 27: 1–28.

3

Exploring Menopause Transition in the Workplace

Carol Atkinson, Jo Duberley and Catrina Page

In this chapter, we explore menopause transition in the workplace. Menopause describes the cessation of periods and is a natural life stage. Menopause transition, or 'peri-menopause', is 'the time between onset of menstrual irregularity and the menopause' (O'Neill and Eden, 2017, p 303).[1] It is associated with a number of symptoms, usually experienced between the ages of 45–55, which include hot flushes, night sweats, mood changes, poor concentration, memory loss, anxiety and weight gain. How each woman experiences menopause transition is different and unique (Banks, 2019) and the impact, duration, onset and severity of symptoms experienced vary greatly. Nevertheless, evidence suggests that, for many, transition symptoms have a negative effect on working lives (Griffiths and Hunter, 2014), with nearly 40 per cent of those in transition agreeing that menopausal symptoms had some negative effect on their work performance (Griffiths, Maclennan and Hassard, 2013). Indeed, a recent study suggests that up to a quarter of those experiencing serious symptoms have left employment (Powell, 2021).

There are a number of reasons why this workplace impact should concern employers, drawing on legal, business and social justice cases (Atkinson et al, 2021). Legally, organizations have a responsibility to employees in menopause transition. They need, for example, to ensure compliance with both the Equality Act 2010 and Health and Safety at Work Act 1974 and ensure they are aware of 'best practice' guidelines. Employer failure to recognize the impact of menopause in the workplace has resulted in a number of employer losses at employment tribunal on the grounds of discrimination and unfair dismissal. The first was recorded in 2012 (Merchant vs BT) and, while numbers are still small, cases brought had grown to ten in the first half of 2021 (Hill, 2021). There is also clearly a strong business case: the workforce is ageing and it is estimated that there are 4.3 million workers who identify as cis women aged between 50–64 in the UK workforce (ONS, 2019). Given that the average age of menopause is 51, a significant number will be working while in transition (O'Neill and Eden, 2017). In July 2017, the UK Government published research on menopause transition (Brewis et al, 2017) and, while they noted that its economic impact is hard to quantify, the figures we have provided on impairment to workplace performance and exit suggest that it is a matter of substantial organizational concern. Ensuring workers are supported during transition is especially important as many are reaching the peak of their work performance and have extensive and valuable knowledge and skills that employers do not wish to lose. Finally, interest around menopause in the workplace has been growing (Atkinson, Carmichael and Duberley, 2021), alongside the social justice case that organizational practice should promote fairness and prioritize well-being and that firms that fail to do so may face negative consequences (Cassar and Buttigieg, 2015). Supporting those in menopause transition is simply the right thing to do.

Once a taboo subject, there has been a recent increase of news items aimed at opening up the conversation around menopause. This has been accompanied by an increase in academic research that suggests that not acknowledging menopause creates an 'inhospitable environment … where menopause is an embarrassing or inappropriate topic' (Jack et al, 2016, p 92). This chapter forms part of the movement that shines a light on organizational practice and recommends ways forward. We report on data that was collected via an online survey between March 2018 and November 2019 from 14 organizations across a range of sectors (including law enforcement; telecommunications; education; legal services and software development). 1,523 responses were collected: 88% (1,343) of participants self-identified as female and 73 per cent were aged over 46. We recognize the sensitivities around language and need for inclusivity in menopause discussion and use gender-neutral language for those in transition, other than where we are quoting our participants or researchers, where we adopt the terms they used. Over 5,000 responses to both closed and open-ended questions were uploaded to data analysis software (Excel and NVivo 11 respectively). Qualitative responses were coded into themes and these, plus supporting quotes, are presented in what follows, alongside descriptive statistics, where appropriate, that indicate weight of evidence.

In what follows, we explore awareness and experiences of menopause symptoms and their workplace impact using the psychological contract as a lens through which to explore the implications for the employment relationship. We discuss issues that influence (non) disclosure of menopausal status and normalizing the conversation around menopause. We also discuss the role of line manager and organizational practice in supporting those in menopause transition. Finally, we conclude with required organizational support and the implications of our discussions of menopause transition for psychological contracts.

Menopause and the employment relationship

We use the psychological contract as a framework to explore the employment relationship. This is an 'individual's belief, shaped by the organisation, regarding terms of exchange agreement between individuals and their organisation' (Rousseau, 1995, p 9). It provides a lens through which to view the sensemaking process, that is, 'the ways in which individuals understand, interpret and create meaning based on information available to them' (Diehl and Coyle-Shapiro, 2019, p 186), and to reflect how those in transition understand the implications of their menopausal status in the workplace. Organizations, HR departments and line managers must ensure consistent and clear communication of their promises and obligations to ensure strong psychological contracts (Guest and Conway, 2002) and we outline later types of organizational help and support that might be appropriate to those in transition. Employees learn a lot about what to expect in terms of the mutual promises and obligations from their organization through implicit and explicit forms of communication and by observing behaviour and attitudes displayed by line managers (Rousseau, 1995) and again we outline a range of attitudes, both positive and negative, in relation in menopause symptoms.

Help and support around menopause transition will underpin a positive psychological contract, leading employees to perceive that the organization cares for their well-being (Eisenberger et al, 1986) and creating perceptions of fairness and justice (Robinson, Kraatz and Rousseau, 1994) and trust in management (Zhao et al, 2007). Perceived organizational support and demonstrating concern for employees' well-being predicts psychological contract fulfilment (Tekleab, Takeuchi and Taylor, 2005), and where employees perceive their employer has fulfilled their psychological contract there is a positive association with both motivational (reduced turnover intentions, work engagement, commitment) and mental health related outcomes (Parzefall and Hakanen, 2010). Furthermore, where employees perceive their organization has exceeded their obligations, this has been shown to have a significant positive effect on the mood dimension of depression–enthusiasm (Conway and Briner, 2002). Conversely, poor line manager support and attitudes may lead those in transition to feel that the organization has breached the psychological contract, that is, it has failed to keep its promises and fulfil its obligations (Guest and Conway, 2002). It has been argued that, where managers do not have the appropriate knowledge, skills or attitudes, they can 'inadvertently increase embarrassment and reinforce stigma' of those in transition (Hardy, Griffiths and Hunter, 2017, p 40). Where employees believe that organizations have promised to treat them fairly and equitably (Guest and Conway, 1998) but subsequent behaviour and attitudes contradict these beliefs, for example overhearing jokes, witnessing derogatory comments or being subjected to negative behaviour and attitudes when in transition, is likely to be perceived as a breach of the psychological contract and result in mistrust in management (Zhao et al, 2007) and negative perceptions of equity and fairness (Robinson, Kraatz and Rousseau, 1994; Rousseau, 1995). We consider these issues in relation to menopause transition in the workplace, and conclude with implications for the psychological contract.

Menopause symptoms and their workplace impact

The range of menopause symptoms recognized by participants was wide-ranging and similar across menopausal and non-menopausal groups. Most common were hot flushes, mood swings, fatigue and weight gain. Less well-known symptoms were associated with loss of libido, pain, headaches, and sleep problems. Other symptoms noted related to poor concentration, memory loss, depression, and anxiety. Almost all of those in menopause transition were aware of at least three menopause symptoms (93 per cent), while amongst others, almost all noted at least one symptom and nearly three-quarters were able to list at least three symptoms. There was then general awareness of menopause symptoms.

Less apparent was an understanding of the severity of symptoms and the impact on work life for those in transition. Contrary to previous research where menopause symptoms were not reported to have an impact on work performance (Hickey et al, 2017), 60 per cent of participants in menopause transition felt it had a moderate impact, and a third a very high impact, on their work tasks and roles. Relatively fewer line managers reported that menopause symptoms might have a very high impact on work, although they had similar perceptions to those in menopause transition of low and moderate impact scores. Responses from those self-identifying as male ($n=$ 156) suggested a lower awareness. This may be because those in transition did not disclose their menopausal status, which we discuss in more detail later, but may also reflect the sample composition. This was weighted towards those who were already experiencing menopause symptoms and were, therefore, more aware of their impact. Symptoms thus appeared to have a significant impact on the work performance of those in menopause transition, even where this was concealed from their line managers (Kittell, Mansfield and Voda, 1998).

Our findings highlighted that those in transition often made extra effort to compensate or 'overcome' their difficulties (Griffiths, Maclennan and Hassard, 2013; Kittell, Mansfield and Voda, 1998): 'I started to perform badly at work as a result of forgetfulness and loss of confidence and lack of structure, which I was appraised negatively on. Now I know I'm menopausal I am having to work harder to overcome the record and excel.'

There is growing evidence to suggest that the impact of the menopause at work is not uni-directional. That is, poor experiences and lack of appropriate support at work might negatively impact on menopause symptoms rather than, simply, menopause symptoms negatively impacting on work performance (Atkinson et al, 2021; Grandey, Gabriel and King, 2020; Reynolds, 1999). Certainly, those in transition reported negative consequences for both their health and careers as a result of 'bending their bodies to organisational norms' (Grandey, Gabriel and King, 2020, p 8). In order to cope, many revealed they had either changed roles or taken sick leave, which had significant impact on their career, or moved out of the workplace altogether:

'I was given a very complex project to deal with and found it very hard to cope due to my severe menopausal symptoms (brain fog, anxiety, insomnia). I approached my then manager on numerous occasions to say that I needed help and that I was really struggling, but she just laughed it off. She couldn't seem to understand that my menopause was really affecting my ability to do my job. I ended up going sick for two months with stress.'

Our data reveal a fair level of awareness of menopause symptoms, together with, in many cases, substantial impact on workplace experiences and job performance. They also suggest that symptoms can be exacerbated by workplace experiences.

Disclosure of menopausal status

Our findings support previous studies that evidence reluctance to disclose symptoms or 'edit out' daily struggles for fear of discrimination, ridicule and prejudice in the workplace (Putnam and Bochantin, 2009; Reynolds, 1999; Griffiths, Maclennan and Hassard, 2013). The fear of being labelled incompetent or 'past it' led to hiding, masking and concealing of symptoms (Kittell, Mansfield and Voda, 1998). Qualitative responses suggested that those in transition often avoided discussing their menopausal status and actively hid their symptoms from colleagues and line managers. Reluctance to disclose was also reflected in reported levels of confidence in discussing menopause symptoms at work. We found those in transition reported the lowest confidence, 43 per cent indicating very low confidence, compared to only 27 per cent of line managers. Perhaps surprisingly, line managers reported the highest confidence in discussing menopause symptoms, with almost 30 per cent reporting very high confidence, compared to only 21 per cent of those in transition.

While male colleagues and line managers, male and female, were most often mentioned as a barrier to open communication and understanding of menopause in the workplace, there were also references to age as a barrier, with a number of participants reporting negative experiences with younger female colleagues and line managers:

'When the emails came out about this [menopause] forum, I was disgusted to hear young women in my office saying, "Look, have you seen this email, just another excuse to get an afternoon off and give someone something to do as a job?" and that the women should just get on with it. I couldn't believe my ears.'

Griffiths, Maclennan and Hassard (2013) identified similar findings, suggesting 42 per cent did not disclose their menopausal status because their line manager was male and 15 per cent because their line manager was younger. Concealment in another study led to 'isolating, silencing and embarrassing [those in transition] … rather than looking for ways to adapt the environment to their needs' (Kittell, Mansfield and Voda, 1998, p 631).

Perhaps unsurprisingly, our data indicate that disclosure and seeking support were related to the extent to which those in transition felt their symptoms were impacting on their job performance. Those who did not seek support from either colleagues, managers or HR departments rated the average impact of menopause on their work ability at 54 (out of 100). Those who sought support from HR departments had an average rating of impact at work of 59, which increased to 61 for colleagues and 64 when disclosing and seeking support from managers. This suggests that seeking support is related to severity of symptoms and perhaps no longer being able to hide the impact on their work. This outweighed the fear or embarrassment associated with disclosure:

'Instead, like me, you feel you have to hide your emotions and symptoms in fear of having them misunderstood or having a negative effect on your role. Holding seminars and forums etc is all very good, but there needs to be a clear structure on how issues are dealt with to instil confidence in both supervisors and the individual it affects.'

Participants were clear, however, that disclosure should be optional, not mandatory, particularly where menopause was framed as a personal problem to be managed by the individual (Putnam and Bochantin, 2009):

'I think we need to be careful that we don't give the impression that these issues HAVE to be discussed – as with any health condition it is private and personal and not something that has to be raised. We have to be careful to strike a balance here and ensure that the awareness training does not give rise to increased unconscious bias.'

Very often the continued struggle with symptoms, coupled with the inability to discuss them openly, resulted in those in transition suffering mental health issues such as anxiety, depression and a loss of confidence. These feelings were also exacerbated as they manifest as both symptoms and consequences.

Embarrassment

In line with other studies (Hardy et al, 2018; Jack, Riach and Bariola, 2019; Griffiths, Maclennan and Hassard, 2013; Reynolds, 1999), those in transition identified their own embarrassment and the possible embarrassment of others as a major barrier to disclosure. This was closely related to concern over how those in transition felt others would perceive them. We know from social psychology literature that individuals will go to great lengths to avoid embarrassment and the associated threat to their social image and identity (Miller, 2007). Perceptions and evaluations of embarrassing situations are intensified when coupled with a fear of negative assessments by others (Miller, 2007). While self-awareness can protect the individual as it 'provides a way for people to make reasoned guesses about other people's thoughts and feelings including their thoughts and feelings about us' (Leary, 2004, p 131), it can also mean individuals fail to appraise the situation accurately or take necessary action (Miller, 2007). Griffiths, Maclennan and Hassard (2013: 159) noted 'managers cannot provide support or offer suitable adjustments if they are not made aware of the problems'.

However, encouraging open and constructive dialogue is not without problems. These in part stem from a wider culture that has stigmatized both ageing and, by association, menopause (Atkinson et al, 2021; Chrisler, 2013, Putnam and Bochantin, 2009). They also result from differential experiences of menopause symptoms, ranging from extremely debilitating to mildly bothersome symptoms, to some in transition even feeling energized (Hardy et al, 2019; Kittell, Mansfield and Voda, 1998). For line managers, there was also concern that navigating or pre-empting a conversation around menopause may be perceived as unduly sensitive or a negative reflection on performance.

These concerns were central to discomfort around menopause conversations and indeed resulted in avoidance of them.

Fear of discrimination and workplace incivility

Disclosure was also reduced by fear of discrimination (Atkinson and Carter, 2018; Griffiths, Maclennan and Hassard, 2013; Reynolds, 1999). There was evidence from our study that those in transition experienced 'gendered ageism' (Atkinson, Carmichael and Duberley, 2021) which impacted on their intentions to disclose their status:

> 'I approached my manager with a light conversation to let him know how I was feeling. … He was clearly embarrassed, would refer to me as a "dried up old bag" in a "joking" manner … I never mentioned my situation again.
>
> I didn't feel able to discuss it as comments were openly made about older women being "menopausal" in a derogatory manner.'

However, it was not simply fear of discrimination that those in transition experienced; rather, they reported numerous acts of workplace incivility. Workplace incivility has been defined as 'low intensity deviant behaviours with ambiguous intent to harm' (Andersson and Pearson, 1999, p 456) where individuals act without regard or respect for others against the expected norms of the organization. Examples abounded and included 'rude comments, thoughtless acts, or negative gestures' (as per Herschcovis et al, 2017, p 453) from both colleagues and managers: 'In a male dominated environment, the menopause can be seen as "women's problems" and not openly discussed or if it is – it just encourages sniggering and eye rolling.

Research indicates that where workplace incivility is experienced, especially where the perpetrator holds a more powerful status (for example line manager), it exacerbates feelings of embarrassment and isolation and has an impact on somatic symptoms such as sleeplessness and headaches (Herschcovis et al, 2017). The consequences for those in our study were significant including, changing roles, taking (un- or under-explained) sick leave, leaving their jobs and, in some cases, feeling suicidal:

> 'At times my moods have been so low, I have been suicidal with hormone imbalance [and] wanted to walk out an 18-year career due to lack of support by management and team-mates.

I went through the menopause early. I didn't want to highlight it at work as I worked in a male dominated team who were older and you just don't talk about these things … I just struggled on to the point I ended up going off work with stress.'

Even where outright discrimination is not evident, organizations need to recognize that workplace incivility can lead to significant negative outcomes, and can be both 'socially isolating and embarrassing' as well as affecting workers' 'well-being' (Herschcovis et al, 2017, p 1070). The quotes that follow illustrate some of the negative attitudes towards menopause reported by line managers.

'[It] needs careful management to ensure those need support get it, but those using it as an excuse are properly managed. Reasonable adjustments need to be available, but care should be taken not to molly-coddle.'

'No to reasonable adjustments – we just wouldn't have a workforce – it isn't a disability like a lot of conditions. It's something we need to be open about and deal with.'

'I hope this doesn't become another reason for certain individuals to skive.'

Where embarrassment is related to the experience of previous negative experiences or fear of negative evaluations, organizations need to make it clear that workplace incivility is not to be tolerated. A whole range of issues then discouraged disclosure and created a tendency to conceal menopause status. We next discuss how this might be addressed and menopause become a comfortable topic of conversation at work.

Normalizing the conversation

Attempts to normalize the conversation (Putnam and Bochantin, 2009) are important to encouraging disclosure and reducing embarrassment, discrimination and fear of workplace incivility (Atkinson, Carmichael and Duberley, 2021). Indeed, 98 per cent of our participants felt it was highly or extremely important to normalize menopause at work. The vast majority were keen to reduce stigma in order to ensure open and transparent discussion:

'The starting point is to be able to facilitate a discussion in one to one sessions with line managers about symptoms that are, or perceived to be, impacting on my ability to get my work done. Better understanding and flexibility and to be made [aware] that the support[is there], if needed.'

We found interesting differences between line managers and those in transition in relation to their perceptions of the extent to which menopause was acknowledged in the workplace. More than half (54 per cent) of those in transition felt that menopause was not acknowledged, compared to 42 per cent of line managers. Across all participants, about half felt that menopause was not acknowledged at all, which perhaps supports the view that HR departments are failing to recognize the importance of menopause in the workplace (Atkinson et al, 2021). This is especially problematic when we consider the bi-directional relationship noted by Atkinson et al (2021) and that a lack of line manager and organizational support can exacerbate menopause symptoms (Kittell, Mansfield and Voda, 1998).

Putnam and Bochantin (2009) have suggested that where menopause is reframed as an organizational concern, as opposed to an individual's problem, this has enabled more effective negotiation of solutions. There is also evidence to suggest that discussing personal problems with colleagues and line managers leads to increased work performance and job satisfaction (Clark, 2002). This does, however, require an open culture that helps those in transition to overcome their own embarrassment and self-consciousness (Miller, 2007) as disclosure is more likely when those in transition feel their supervisors and colleagues are more informed and empathetic and when they themselves have a more positive attitude (Reynolds, 1999). Indeed, where those in transition do disclose their status to managers, the support they receive is highly valued (Griffiths, Maclennan and Hassard, 2013: 159). From qualitative responses, there was evidence that open discussion significantly helped those in transition cope with their symptoms. They felt more supported and understood. The understanding and awareness gained through open discussion allowed for consideration of workplace modification which improved both performance and mental health:

'My worst year was last year when I was constantly feeling nauseous, had headaches, terrible mood swings and literally just felt awful. I was able to connect with my manager at this time who was going through a similar stage and immediately knew where I was at and how I felt. This in turn made me feel so much better.

For me, being open and honest about how I feel has helped enormously and encourages other colleagues to talk about it too.'

Suggestions about how to normalize the conversation included explicit policies and practices related to acceptable workplace behaviour, bullying, and anti-discrimination law. Normalizing the conversation was also achieved through awareness raising and training, increasing the likelihood of 'perspective taking' (Madera, Neal and Dawson, 2011), which has been shown to have a significant impact on attitudes and empathy towards others (Stocks et al, 2011).

Role of line managers

ACAS (2022) stresses the importance of managers, supervisors and team leaders receiving training to enable them to have open conversations about perimenopause or menopause. ACAS also outlines guidance that includes encouraging an environment where discussion of menopause is supported, increasing awareness of menopause, ensuring company policies are available and well-publicized and urging organizations to consider 'having a menopause or well-being champion' instead of treating it as a taboo subject or a personal matter (also see Matthews, 2015; Hardy et al, 2019). Altmann (2015) argues that line managers in particular require training in how to support those experiencing the menopause. Line managers play an important role in developing a supportive culture where discussion of menopausal status and agreement of appropriate adjustments is possible (Matthews, 2015; Hardy et al, 2019). They also play a crucial role in implementing HR policy as organizations increasingly devolve HR responsibilities (Leisink and Knies, 2011; Huo, Boxall and Cheung, 2020). In addition, they are the channel through which employees understand their relationship with their organization (Hui, Lee and Rousseau, 2004). Supportive line managers have a positive impact on well-being (Huo, Boxall and Cheung, 2020) and, additionally, social support provided by line managers has a role in buffering negative job stressors (Schreurs et al, 2012).

Line managers therefore require training in how to provide both formal and informal support (Hardy et al, 2018; Altmann, 2015). Indeed, line manager responses in our study suggested they required support not only in terms of awareness training, but also in terms of the specific skills in *how* to discuss menopause confidently and sensitively (Hardy et al, 2019). While, as discussed earlier, some line managers felt confident in discussing menopause, this was not the norm. The evidence suggested a polarized response; there were as many line managers who reported very low confidence as there were who reported very high confidence in managing discussions around menopause. Almost 30 per cent of line managers felt they had little to no confidence in discussing menopause:

'as a line manager there appears to be no support available and not knowing who to contact or where to look.'

'I am a line manager and have absolutely no idea about the menopause which perhaps says a lot.'

'I shamefully don't really know a lot about the menopause … so a better understanding and awareness is needed so that it can be managed empathetically and supportively within my role.'

Our findings suggest that almost all line managers believed that it is necessary to educate managers. Three-quarters of line managers would like to be able to openly discuss the menopause at work without embarrassment and for organizations to run menopause awareness programmes for all employees.

'As a male manager of a largely female team, I need to understand how menopause may impact on performance and relationships in the team so that I don't misinterpret things. Being able to discuss it openly in the workplace will hopefully remove barriers and embarrassment so that there is greater understanding of the difficulties menopause presents to individuals.'

There was, again, general consensus that no one should be forced to disclose their menopausal status, however many line managers recognized a need to deepen their understanding in order to deal with this issue sensitively should anyone wish to discuss it.

As noted, the overwhelming reason for women failing to seek support was their own embarrassment, together with the perceived embarrassment of others. However, it should also be considered that those in transition might be overestimating the negative perceptions of line managers. Out of 1,525 responses, 689 individuals included further comments regarding their own experiences, suggestions and thoughts. Of these, 130 individuals made specific reference to managers, line managers or supervisors. On closer analysis, 19 described specific examples of positive support, 12 reported negative experiences and 3 discussed both positive and negative exchanges. The remaining 96 comments described reticence and perceptions related to feeling unable to discuss menopause with managers due to concerns over their own embarrassment and the possible embarrassment of their manager. Typical comments included:

'Not discussed it with anyone – line managers are all male – not comfortable raising the issue. Don't think they would be comfortable either' 'I don't want to talk about it but I would like to be understood. I think male colleagues will not take the matter seriously'.

While a mixed picture emerges, it is nevertheless clear that line managers require support in opening supportive discussions around menopause symptoms.

Help and support for those in transition

Due to varying experiences of symptoms, not all those in transition will need support. However, according to our findings, 60 per cent of those in transition were not accessing or able to access support in the workplace. When asked about sources of support, the other 40 per cent said they had received support from either a colleague, manager, HR or occupational health (OH). Of those in transition, 27 per cent had approached a colleague for support and 15 per cent had sought support from a manager. However, significantly fewer (4 per cent) sought support from either HR or OH. The fear of being judged negatively, coupled with the stress of masking and hiding symptoms meant most of those in transition paradoxically fail to seek help and support in obtaining the adjustments needed to cope (Grandey, Gabriel and King, 2020).

Of those that sought support from workplace sources, experiences were both positive and negative. Where the experience was positive, it was closely linked to awareness and open communication, supporting earlier evidence presented that open, honest discussion of menopause was critical to better outcomes in the workplace:

'I have been extremely lucky to have a knowledgeable understanding line manager who has been able to put things in place for me to manage my day to day duties.

I was, and still am, experiencing severe fatigue and insomnia, which was having an adverse effect on my memory and ability to organise myself. My line manager suggested that I start work a little bit later for a few weeks, and I found this really helpful. There was no pressure from my line manager and I have found her really supportive.'

Where negative experiences were described, they had a long-lasting impact and significant impact:

'I started having symptoms just after I stepped into a senior role, unfortunately they impacted my ability to perform. My manager lost patience with me and I felt bullied as he continuously criticised me. I was moved out of my role and my confidence was depleted.'

When asked what organizations might do to support menopause in the workplace, over 80 per cent of participants wanted menopause to be part of a company well-being programme. Almost three-quarters of participants felt that managers should be educated, slightly fewer (68 per cent) wanted the organization to run an awareness programme for all. Around 65 per cent and 64 per cent, respectively, wanted introduction of reasonable adjustments and to be able to discuss menopause openly and without embarrassment. While this suggests more than a third of participants don't want open discussion or reasonable adjustments, this may be related to a lack of awareness of the impact of menopausal symptoms and the fear that open discussion might be embarrassing or further 'problematise and possibly marginalise women unless very sensitively handled' (Jack et al, 2014, p 25).

In addition to closed questions, participants were asked to offer further suggestions regarding how their organization might support menopausal workers. A total of 136 participants responded to this question with various suggestions. The majority of responses were related to promoting understanding (69), including simple acknowledgement, open discussion, training and education in order to raise awareness and reduce stigma of menopause in the workplace. Additional suggestions included offering flexible working, provision of desk fans and control of air-con, adequate toilets and sanitary provision, adjustments and alternatives to uniforms and better policy and guidelines regarding the kinds of reasonable adjustments that could be made. Several responses suggested different formal and informal support groups might be offered.

Many participants thus articulated a desire for practices outlined by Jack et al (2016, p 93): 'providing health promotion programmes, information and support, and awareness raising and sensitivity training for managers, and generating a positive cultural environment for menopausal women at work'. However, in our study, there were others who were clearly wary, confused and in some cases openly hostile to the suggestion that those in transition might require help and support, or reasonable adjustments to their work practices. For example, while 70 per cent of line managers agreed it was necessary to introduce reasonable adjustments for menopause symptoms in the workplace, nearly a third of line managers did not:

'I have concerns that in a majority male working environment, highlighting menopausal symptoms could be used against women: I can imagine an interviewer preferring a male candidate to a menopausal woman.'

'I wouldn't want menopause to become an excuse for me although I do use it in jest when I make some mistakes. I think it is a taboo subject that a lot of male colleagues don't understand: they just steer clear of the conversation.'

If this is a pervasive issue and our survey is indicative of wider sentiment, this might lead to costly and distressing employment tribunals for both employers and employees. We suggest that urgent education is required to make clear the legal requirements set out in the Equality Act 2010. Ensuring those in transition are supported is especially important as many are reaching the peak of their work performance and have extensive and valuable knowledge and skills that employers do not wish to lose. This study adds to growing evidence (Brewis et al, 2017) that those in transition may leave their jobs as a result of an unsupportive environment:

'Most of us who are menopausal are long-term employees so our experience/knowledge etc of the job are important and we should be managed accordingly.'

'I left a management job … a few years ago due to my menopause. … Now I have come back to the organisation at a lower grade so that I can manage a work life [balance].'

Implications of managing menopause in the workplace for the employment relationship

In this section, we present our findings in relation to line manager/ organization support and the willingness of those in transition to disclose their status (Figure 3.1). We then return to our earlier discussion of the psychological contract to draw out the implications of our findings for the employment relationship.

Figure 3.1 outlines the benefits of organizational support and an environment that facilitates disclose of menopausal status. As we have evidenced in this chapter, organization/line manager failure to live up to organizational obligations to support equality, fairness, and justice

Figure 3.1: Women's experiences related to willingness to disclose and support available

High	Positive organizational policies and practices (HR and OH) – opportunity to access reasonable adjustments	One to one support – opportunity to discuss individual reasonable adjustments
	Formal and informal education and awareness programmes for all staff	Informal and formal groups, e.g. menopause cafes, women's support networks, well-being officers
Organizational/ line manager support	Flexible working, ventilation, provision of appropriate toilet and sanitary facilities	Provision of desk fans, lightweight or alternative uniforms
	Avoiding	Taboo – Ignored, dismissed, not taken seriously
	Hiding, masking, concealment	
Low	Increased stress, somatic and vasomoter symptoms	Discrimination, ridicule, workplace incivility
	Undisclosed sickness/absence, etc.	Turnover intentions, increased sickness/absence, etc.
	No/Closed	Yes/Open

Willingness to disclose

can have negative consequences, leading to breach of the psychological contract. Those in transition experiencing stigma, or ridicule related to their symptoms, is a clear example of this and had anticipated negative impact on work-related outcomes including organizational commitment, job satisfaction, turnover intentions, organizational citizenship behaviours, in-role performance and well-being (Conway, Guest and Trenberth, 2011, Zhao et al, 2007):

'The feeling of isolation, loss of confidence contributed to me handing in my [notice] along with a throw away comment from a male manager who would be totally unaware of the impact this had.'

'I started having symptoms just after I stepped into a senior role, unfortunately they impacted my ability to perform. My manager lost patience with me and I felt bullied as he continuously criticised me. I was moved out of my role and my confidence was depleted. Sadly, although my menopause is under control, I don't have the confidence any more to progress at work. I feel trapped in a job that I can do very well, I know I am capable of doing more but I lack the self-belief and confidence to aim higher.'

The concept of breach helps us understand how those in transition make sense of a negative event, and how this might subsequently lead to feelings of injustice (Conway, Guest and Trenberth, 2011) or how it might impact their intentions to disclose their status, or seek adjustments to help alleviate their symptoms (Chaudhry, Wayne and Schalk, 2009). Managers 'can alleviate the negative impact of breach by paying closer attention to employee's emotional states and putting out the "fire" before negative behaviour occurs' (Zhao et al, 2007, p 671). However, other studies suggest that, once breached, the psychological contract is difficult to repair especially if the employee feels they have fulfilled their side of the promise (Conway, Guest and Trenberth, 2011). This might particularly be the case, for example, where those in transition feel they have worked harder to compensate for the effects of menopause symptoms, as has been reported elsewhere (Atkinson, Carmichael and Duberley, 2021). Addressing the knowledge gap, opening up the discussion, and normalizing the conversation could ensure that breach does not happen in the first place. For example:

'I was, and still am, experiencing severe fatigue and insomnia, which was having an adverse effect on my memory and ability to organise myself. My line manager suggested that I start work a little bit later for a few weeks, and I found this really helpful. There was no pressure from my line manager and I have found her really supportive.'

However, if organizations fail to adopt policies that support those in transition and facilitate appropriate line manager behaviour, they risk misunderstandings and misinterpretations which can be costly in terms of breach of the psychological contract, poor performance, negative behaviours, and most seriously discrimination claims (Cassar and Buttigieg, 2015).

Conclusions

Across this chapter, we have explored how menopause transition is experienced in the workplace. We evidence that, for many, it creates substantial challenges and that, while awareness is growing, there is a long way to go in creating open and supportive workplaces in which those in transition receive the support necessary to survive and thrive in their roles. Indeed, there were over one hundred references in our data to embarrassment, shame, stigma and taboo, perhaps explaining why non-disclosure of menopausal status is so high. This suggests that substantial culture change in organizations is needed to normalize the conversation around menopause. Given the bi-directional nature of menopause symptoms, that is, where a lack of organizational support can exacerbate symptoms, it becomes imperative to increase appropriate training for line managers in order to build their confidence around discussing menopause. This in turn enables them to better support those in transition. Using a psychological contract framework, we outline the importance of effective support for those in menopause transition and how this can positively, or negatively, impact important outcomes such as organizational commitment, job satisfaction, turnover intentions, organizational citizenship behaviours, in-role performance and well-being. It is essential that organizations retain older workers as a valuable labour resource, and we conclude this chapter with some suggestions for actions that will support this.

As we note, culture change is needed and we recognize that this is an inevitably slow process. Nevertheless, a starting point is awareness raising around menopause, perhaps via workshops, seminars or intranet sites, and training for line managers in how to open up supportive conversations and offer adjustments required. Clear and accessible policies and procedures or toolkits will be an important part of this. Menopause transition should be thus positioned as an organizational, not individual, concern and dealt with accordingly. Practical interventions are also an important part of support and can include flexible working, provision of desk fans and control of air-con, adequate toilets and sanitary provision, adjustments and alternatives to uniforms. Well-being champions or other mechanisms of formal or informal support can also be very effective. Awareness of these mechanisms and the ability to access them is vitally important. Interventions can thus be wide-ranging but must be championed at a senior level if they are to have sufficient weight to change culture and create a supportive workplace environment in which those in menopause transition can retain their dignity and confidence and continue in their chosen employment. Given the ageing workforce demographic, organizations will ignore this at their peril.

Note

[1] Please note that transition as used in this chapter refers only to menopause and not to the various forms of medical and social gender transition which transgender and other gender-diverse people experience.

References

ACAS (2022) *Menopause at Work*, [online] https://www.acas.org.uk/menopause-at-work/supporting-staff-through-the-menopause [Accessed 27 June 2022].

Altmann, R. (2015) *A New Vision for Older Workers: Retain, Retrain, Recruit*, London: Department for Work and Pensions.

Andersson, L. and Pearson, C. (1999) 'Tit for tat? The spiraling effect of incivility in the workplace', *Academy of Management Review*, 24(3): 452–71.

Atkinson, C., Beck, V., Brewis, J., Davies, A. and Duberley, J. (2021) 'Menopause and the workplace: New directions in HR research and practice', *Human Resource Management Journal*, 31(1): 49–64.

Atkinson, C., Carmichael, F. and Duberley, J. (2021) 'The menopause taboo: Examining women's embodied experiences of menopause in the UK police service', *Work, Employment and Society*, 35(4): 657–76.

Atkinson, C. and Carter, J. (2018). *Menopause in the Workplace: West Yorkshire Police*, [online] https://www2.mmu.ac.uk/media/mmuacuk/content/documents/business-school/decent-work-and-productivity/WY-Police-Menopause-Report.pdf [Accessed 28 October 2019].

Banks, S. (2019) 'Menopause and the NHS: Caring for and retaining the older workforce', *British Journal of Nursing*, 28(16): 1086–90.

Brewis, J., Beck, V., Davies, A. and Matheson, J. (2017) *The Impact of Menopause Transition on Women's Economic Participation in the UK*, [online] 20 July. Available from: https://www.gov.uk/government/publications/menopause-transition-effects-on-womens-economic-participation [Accessed 17 November 2022].

Cassar, V. and Buttigieg, S. (2015) 'Psychological contract breach, organizational justice and emotional well-being', *Personnel Review*, 44(2): 217–235.

Chaudhry, A., Wayne, S. and Schalk, R. (2009) 'A sensemaking model of employee evaluation of psychological contract fulfillment: When and how do employees respond to change?' *The Journal of Applied Behavioral Science*, 45(4): 498–520.

Chrisler, J. (2013) 'Teaching taboo topics: Menstruation, menopause, and the psychology of women', *Psychology of Women Quarterly*, 37(1): 128–32.

Clark, S. (2002) 'Communicating across the work/home border', *Community, Work & Family*, 5(1): 23–48.

Conway, N. and Briner, R. (2002) 'A daily diary study of affective responses to psychological contract breach and exceeded promises', *Journal of Organizational Behavior*, 23(3): 287–302.

Conway, N., Guest, D. and Trenberth, L. (2011) 'Testing the differential effects of changes in psychological contract breach and fulfillment', *Journal of Vocational Behavior*, 79(1): 267–276.

Diehl, M.-R. and Coyle-Shapiro, J.A-M. (2019) 'Psychological contracts through the lens of sensemaking', in Griep, Y. and Cooper, C. (eds) *Handbook of Research on the Psychological Contract at Work*, Cheltenham: Edward Elgar, pp 186–205.

Eisenberger, R., Huntingdon, R., Hutchison, S. and Sowa, D. (1986) 'Perceived organizational support', *Journal of Applied Psychology*, 71(3): 500–7.

Grandey, A., Gabriel, A. and King, E. (2020) 'Tackling taboo topics: A review of the three Ms in working women's lives', *Journal of Management*, 46(1): 7–35.

Griffiths, A. and Hunter, M. (2014) 'Psychosocial factors and menopause: The impact of menopause on personal and working life', in Davies, S. (ed) *Annual Report of the Chief Medical Officer*, London: Department of Health, pp 109–120. Available from: https://www.gov.uk/government/publications/chief-medical-officer-annual-report-2014-womens-health (Accessed 7 November 2023).

Griffiths, A., Maclennan, S. and Hassard, J. (2013) 'Menopause and work: An electronic survey of employees' attitudes in the UK', *Maturitas*, 76(2): 155–9.

Guest, D. and Conway, N. (1998) *Fairness at Work and the Psychological Contract*, London: Institute of Personnel and Development.

Guest, D. and Conway, N. (2002) 'Communicating the psychological contract: An employer perspective', *Human Resource Management Journal*, 12(2): 22–38.

Hardy, C., Griffiths, A. and Hunter, M. (2017) 'What do working menopausal women want?' *Maturitas*, 101: 37–41.

Hardy, C., Griffiths, A., Thorne, E. and Hunter, M. (2019) 'Tackling the taboo: Talking menopause-related problems at work', *International Journal of Workplace Health Management*, 12(1): 28–38.

Hardy, C., Thorne, E., Griffiths, A. and Hunter, M. (2018) 'Work outcomes in midlife women: The impact of menopause, work stress and working environment', *Women's Midlife Health*, 4(3): 1–8. doi: 10.1186/ s40695-018-0036-z.

Herschcovis, M., Neville, L., Reich, T., Christie, A., Cortina, L. and Shan, J. (2017) 'Witnessing wrongdoing: The effects of observer power on incivility intervention in the workplace', *Organizational Behavior and Human Decision Processes*, 142: 45–57.

Hickey, M., Riach, K., Kachoiue, R. and Jack, G. (2017) 'No sweat: Managing menopausal symptoms at work', *Journal of Psychosomatic Obstetrics and Gynaecology*, 38(3): 202–9.

Hill, A. (2021) 'Menopause at centre of increasing number of UK employment tribunals', *The Guardian*, 7 August. Available from: https://www.theguardian.com/uk-news/2021/aug/07/menopause-centre-increasing-number-uk-employment-tribunals [Accessed 26 July 2023].

Hui, C., Lee, C. and Rousseau, D. (2004) 'Employment relationships in China: Do workers relate to the organization or to people?', *Organization Science*, 15(2): 232–40.

Huo, M., Boxall, P. and Cheung, G. (2020) 'How does line-manager support enhance worker wellbeing? A study in China', *The International Journal of Human Resource Management*, 31(14): 1825–43.

Jack, G., Pitts, M., Riach, K., Bariola, E., Schapper, J. and Sarrel, P. (2014) *Women, Work and the Menopause: Releasing the Potential of Older Professional Women*, [online], September. Available from: https://apo.org.au/node/41511 [Accessed 20 July 2022].

Jack, G., Riach, K. and Bariola, E. (2019) 'Temporality and gendered agency: Menopausal subjectivities in women's work', *Human Relations*, 72(1): 122–43.

Jack, G., Riach, K., Bariola, E., Pitts, M., Schapper, J. and Sarrel, P. (2016) 'Menopause in the workplace: What employers should be doing', *Maturitas*, 85: 88–95.

Kittell, L., Mansfield, P. and Voda, A. (1998) 'Keeping up appearances: The basic social process of the menopausal transition', *Qualitative Health Research*, 8(5): 618–33.

Leary, M. (2004) 'Digging deeper: The fundamental nature of "Self-conscious" emotions', *Psychological Inquiry*, 15(2): 129–31.

Leisink, P. and Knies, E. (2011) 'Line managers' support for older workers', *The International Journal of Human Resource Management*, 22(9): 1902–17.

Madera, J., Neal, J. and Dawson, M. (2011) 'A strategy for diversity training: Focusing on empathy in the workplace', *Journal of Hospitality & Tourism Research*, 35(4): 469–87.

Matthews, V. (2015) 'Managing the change: HR issues', *Occupational Health & Wellbeing*, 67(5): 18.

Miller, R.S. (2007) 'Is embarrassment a blessing or a curse?, in Tracy, J., Robins, R. and Tangney, J. (eds) *The Self-conscious Emotions: Theory and Research*, New York: Guilford Press, pp 245–62.

O'Neill, S. and Eden, J. (2017) 'The pathophysiology of menopausal symptoms', *Obstetrics, Gynaecology & Reproductive Medicine*, 27(10): 303–10.

Office for National Statistics (2019) *Economic Labour Market Status of Individuals Aged 50 and Over, Trends Over Time*, London: Office for National Statistics. Available from: https://assets.publishing.service.gov.uk/media/5d78b65a40f0b61ccdfa4b3c/economic-labour-market-status-of-individuals-aged-50-and-over-sept-2019.pdf [Accessed 26 July 2023].

Parzefall, M. and Hakanen, J. (2010) 'Psychological contract and its motivational and health-enhancing properties', *Journal of Managerial Psychology*, 25(1): 4–21.

Powell, C. (2021) 'Quarter of women with serious menopause symptoms have left jobs, study finds', *People Management*, 18 October. Available from: https://www.peoplemanagement.co.uk/news/articles/quarter-women-with-serious-menopause-symptoms-have-left-jobs?utm_source=mc&utm_medium=email&utm_content=PM_daily_18102021.Quarter+of+women+with+serious+menopause+symptoms+have+left+jobs%2c+study+finds&utm_campaign=7295441&utm_term=5057407#gref [Accessed 26 July 2023].

Putnam, L. and Bochantin, J. (2009) 'Gendered bodies: Negotiating normalcy and support', *Negotiation and Conflict Management Research*, 2(1): 57–73.

Reynolds, F. (1999) 'Distress and coping with hot flushes at work: Implications for counsellors in occupational settings', *Counselling Psychology Quarterly*, 12(4): 353–61.

Robinson, S., Kraatz, M. and Rousseau, D. (1994) 'Changing obligations and the psychological contract: A longitudinal study', *Academy of Management Journal*, 37(1): 137–52.

Rousseau, D. (1995) *Understanding Psychological Contracts*, London: Sage.

Schreurs, B., Van Emmerick, H., Guenter, I. and Germeys, F. (2012) 'A weekly diary study on the buffering role of social support in the relationship between job insecurity and employee performance', *Human Resource Management*, 51(2): 259–79.

Stocks, E., Lishner, D., Waits, B. and Downum, E. (2011) 'I'm embarrassed for you: The effect of valuing and perspective taking on empathic embarrassment and empathic concern', *Journal of Applied Social Psychology*, 41(1): 1–26.

Tekleab, A., Takeuchi, R. and Taylor, M. (2005) 'Extending the chain of relationships among organizational justice, social exchange, and employee reactions: The role of contract violations', *Academy of Management Journal*, 48(1): 146–57.

Zhao, H., Wayne, S., Glibkowski, B. and Bravo, J. (2007) 'The impact of psychological contract breach on work-related outcomes: A meta-analysis', *Personnel Psychology*, 60: 647–80.

4

Workplace Policies, Menopause and Flexible Working: The Need for a More Collective Approach

Jane Parry

Introduction

This chapter considers the poor fit between workplace policy and menopause considerations in UK organizations, coming at these issues through the lens of flexible work and its utilization in workplaces. As the editors and other contributors here have amply demonstrated, for many organizations, policy and practice supporting menopause transitions in the workplace has constituted a blind spot in human resource management (HRM) processes. Rather than explicitly engaging in the issue, managers have tended to approach changing work needs around menopause through a work adjustment process. This is more typical of the way in which organizations have responded to the difficulties that 9–5 office-bound working patterns can pose for older workers, for example, through designing flexible working arrangements or making other adjustments to standardized working patterns. This chapter takes the position that this kind of approach can be inappropriate for a stage in the lifecourse that is fluctuating and variable. Rather, organizational offers around flexible work would be improved through becoming more responsive, and managers more adept at designing and monitoring flexible working arrangements.

Loretto and Vickerstaff (2015) have made the case for adopting a more critical analysis of the role of flexible work in managing older workers, with gender cited as a key differentiator of experiences.

Given the alignment of the average age of menopause at 51 (Brewis et al, 2017) with the 'older worker' category of 50+ frequently used in labour market analysis, it might be expected that menopause is a key component driving women's flexible work requests at this point in their working lives. Indeed, given rising life expectancy and the upward policy manipulation of the state pension age, and the pressures that these place upon older workers to remain active in the workforce well beyond menopause, there is a strong economic imperative for more responsive solutions to be developed around flexible work that can support the extension of working lives. In this chapter, these issues are considered with reference to three separate pieces of research by the author which have resonance for bringing together flexible work around menopause management. The chapter discusses: the visibility of menopause in organizations' HRM discussions; the triggers that prompt employers to get involved in menopause as a workforce issue; the different approaches that organizations are adopting; the adaptive potential of flexible work in supporting employees around menopause; and learnings from the COVID-19 pandemic that can be applied to work organizations around menopause experiences. Together, these enable us to reflect upon what is missing from the current workforce agenda around menopause, as well as who is being excluded from a more supportive employment context around changing working needs related to menopause transitions.

Given the low profile of menopause in current workplace discussions around flexibility, the organizational treatment of women's changing needs around this time arguably have more in common with idiosyncratic deals (Rousseau, Ho and Greenberg, 2006) than a more systematic attempt to provide a baseline of support around menopause that might then be adapted to reflect need. In practice, this represents a drift away from more collectivized manifestations of the psychological contract in which there is reciprocity or agreement around the parties' obligations and contributions (Alcover et al, 2017). This variation in the way that flexible working arrangements are negotiated can present an opportunity for differential or discriminatory treatment to arise, which in menopause can coincide with vulnerabilities around age and gender. It is proposed that the psychological contract around menopause is in its relative infancy in workforce practice, given that discussions around menopause still have a fairly low profile and have not yet been embedded into HRM practice in a consistent way. Thus the contribution being made to discussion here is more along the side of psychological contract *fulfilment*, rather than breach (Karani, Trivedi and Thanki, 2021), given that the latter would suggest a more established set of workforce policy and practice around menopause support than currently exists in most UK workplaces.

This chapter contributes to HRM knowledge by looking at the gap that has emerged between a legislative framework that could potentially support menopause transitions and more routine workplace decision-making that lacks the nuance to accommodate diverse working arrangements. It is argued that intersectional theory offers mileage in developing more effective psychological contracts that acknowledge changing and varied needs associated with menopause and normalize the accommodation of these within workplace practice.

Flexible work and the menopause deficit in human resource management policy

HRM policy, as well as practice, has lagged in its coverage of menopause (Atkinson et al, 2021), at the same time as this has considerable implications for corporate social responsibility, diversity and inclusion, and business development agendas. Demographically, older women workers form a growing component of UK workforces, with numbers of women in the 50–64 age group's employment rate rising by 15 per cent over the past 20 years, while older men's workforce participation rose by 8 per cent over the same period (Centre for Ageing Better, 2020).

The pandemic period has raised concerns about the economic activity of precisely this demographic, with employment rates of older workers falling by twice that of those under 50 over 2020–21 (Cominetti, 2021). This remains an area where further research is needed to understand what prompted the premature labour market exit of older workers where pre-pandemic the opposite effect had been observed. Pressure to return to workplaces in specified ways after a period of working more flexibly (from home, in formerly office-based jobs) is one explanation to be considered. Meanwhile, in key worker jobs, the need to wear PPE and required presence in often unairconditioned workplaces during lockdowns, may have been particularly challenging for workers experiencing menopausal symptoms, and prompted re-evaluation of work priorities. Some indication of the impact that workplace changes can have upon decision-making, is provided by Evandrou et al's (2021) pre-pandemic analysis of NCDS data, which indicated that women experiencing one or more severe menopausal symptoms were more likely to leave jobs or reduce their working hours.

Access to flexible work in the UK has been notably individualized, structured latterly through the extension of the right to request this in the Employment Act in 2014, which places the impetus upon workers to articulate their need for flexible work in terms of a business case terminology, and to negotiate working adjustments on a case-by-case basis with line managers. There is evidence, however, that a more accentuated 'individual accommodation' of flexible work is preferred by employers (Perlow and Kelly, 2014), that is, more informal and *ad hoc* flexible working arrangements (FWAs) should be utilized before formal requests are made around a need for contractual change. This creates a tension between the legal process set out to support flexible work, and more normalized workplace practices. This inconsistency is important because it provides the potential to disempower those who would most benefit from FWAs, particularly if there is perceived to be sensitivity around a request, as for example the evidence suggests there could be in raising the issue of menopause transitions with employers (Griffiths, MacLennan and Hassard, 2013). It is the most vulnerable groups in workplaces who might benefit most from a robust and supportive application process around flexible work.

Flexible work is a generic concept that incorporates a wide range of working practices, which may be drawn upon in relation to different types of demands. Its formats include part-time work, special leave, working from home, job shares, compressed hours, and tapered working, each of which can be manifested differently within workplaces, drawing upon organizational precedents. Indeed, Young (2018) has suggested that there are over 300 variants around flexible work, with hours, location, schedule, contract and structure of jobs being key differentiators. At the heart of flexible work is job design, and applying new solutions to the challenges of diverse workforces and the ever-changing world of work. Given that flexible work has potential for so much adaptability, it is a workplace intervention that offers considerable mileage for people in menopause, whose experiences are diverse and differentiated (Atkinson et al, 2021), and for whom there is no single working arrangement that aligns with their changing working needs.

Flexible work legislation (amended by the 2023 Employment Relations (Flexible Working) Act) already makes provision for time-limited requests to be sought; however, the Department for Business,

Energy and Industrial Strategy (BEIS, 2021) reports that applications of this nature are under-utilized, likely because this aspect of the framework is little publicized and thus general knowledge remains low. Given the uncertainty and variation around menopause experiences, it can be difficult for employees to define in an application the period for which they would like to vary their working arrangements. Tellingly, in the BEIS documentation surrounding the consultation to make flexible work the default (September–December 2021), there is no mention of menopause, which is some indication of the invisibility of menopause transitions in working experiences.

The right to request process that has underpinned legal requests provides a broad framework for incorporating the discourse of flexible work into the UK's labour market. However, workplaces are at different stages of development in terms of flexible working practices, and organizational cultures, in addition to managerial preferences, are a strong influence on access to flexible working arrangements (Parry, 2017). Furthermore, the implementation of the right to request process within organizations can have unequal effects, since applications have required staff competency in deploying a specific business narrative to make their case, which they may not necessarily be familiar nor receive any support with. This is distinct from FWAs forming part of a broader equal opportunities programme, and the need for employees to formulate a distinctive kind of case in order to access them can present an unassailable barrier to potential beneficiaries. It is a requirement that has tended to privilege more valued, higher-status employees (Parry, 2017), a category in which women are underrepresented in the UK's workforce.

The literature has also flagged managerial discussions around menopause as a space that can be unsatisfactory and uncomfortable (Butler, 2020). These might be even more complicated for trans, non-binary and intersex people, where employers' awareness around their menopause experiences is weak. Consequently, the anticipated character of flexible work discussions, in which the impetus is placed upon employees to initiate individualized conversations, underpinned by health and well-being motivations, can be an off-putting aspect of making an application, potentially reducing flexible work requests and creating a barrier around policy implementation.

This particular manifestation of the psychological contract can be compared to an idiosyncratic employment contract or i-deal (Rousseau et al, 2006), whereby employment conditions are negotiated around individual workers' circumstances rather than via a more systematic, organizational-wide approach. While the large proportion of SMEs in the UK's labour market, lacking robust HRM infrastructure, provides some explanation for a reliance upon individualized negotiations around FWAs (Atkinson and Sandiford, 2016), the potential complexity of designing flexible work policy around dynamic workforce needs may also have informed a reliance upon more personalized approaches throughout the labour market (Atkinson, 2020). While it has been suggested that i-deals offer value for heterogeneous older workers with diverse needs (Bal and Jansen, 2015), employees may be more reluctant to draw attention to age-related issues in a labour market where they fear that this might make them vulnerable to redundancy. In this context, women and those who are gender non-conforming or intersex may face intersectional disadvantage around menopause related to age, gender and class.

It is important to highlight the different characteristics of older women's work in analysing these issues. Notably, employment surveys generally classify older workers as those in the 50–64 age bracket, so there is some overlap between menopause experience and this category, although notably menopause can start much earlier. Working women over 50 are three times more likely to be working part time than men in the same age group (Centre for Ageing Better, 2020), and these jobs tend to be of lower quality with reduced access to employment benefits (O'Sullivan, Cross and Lavelle, 2021) such as flexible work – although such access may be masked by part-time work's classification as flexible work when it may be just as fixed as a standard contract. Older women are also more likely to work in particular sectors, such as education and health and social care, than men (CfAB, 2020), fixed working environments in which control over personal space may be limited. The evidence base suggests that what women most want to help manage their menopause symptoms at work is greater flexibility around their working hours and workspaces (Hickey et al, 2017).

This chapter asserts that while informal and idiosyncratic approaches to managing flexible working arrangements have been presented in organizations as a suitable approach for managing diverse and fluctuating workforce needs, there is a potential deficiency in relying upon this kind of psychological contract around menopause. Idiosyncratic approaches neglect to engage with the challenge of reconciling the lack of a dialogue around this issue in many organizations and the sensitivity that is still experienced in raising menopause experiences with line managers. It is argued that shifting back towards a psychological contract with more clearly defined terms and understandings for both parties will be more beneficial at this fairly early stage of embedding good practice around menopause workforce support.

Methods

This chapter draws upon two qualitative projects which focused upon (1) employers' engagement with older workers' flexible work requests, and contextualizes these in a discussion of (2) age-friendly workplaces. The first of these, conducted over the period 2015–16, was qualitative research with, first, policy stakeholders (such as the Department for Work and Pensions, the Advisory, Conciliation and Arbitration Service and the Trades Union Congress), and subsequently staff in a range of positions within case study organizations in the public and charitable sectors, with contrasting flexible work cultures. Qualitative interviews investigated the challenges for employers in managing flexible work requests triggered by the 2014 universalization of the right to request legislation (Parry, 2017). The second project was a mixed-methods piece of research conducted over 2017–18, which involved a rapid evidence review, qualitative interviews and an omnibus employer survey (Smeaton and Parry, 2018). This chapter draws upon the qualitative component of this research: interviews with employers across a range of sectors, intermediaries (such as the Local Government Association and Timewise, a flexible working consultancy), and experts (such as Menopause in the Workplace and the Recruitment and Employment Federation) to explore key aspects of best practice in age-friendly workplaces, of which flexible work was a key factor. Together, these generated 38 transcripts. Both projects were analysed thematically using NVivo (Braun and Clarke, 2006), and coding frameworks were reassessed and text searches conducted, to explore the data in relation to organizational responses to menopause transitions.

Later, the chapter reflects upon how lockdown-driven mass working from home can present an opportunity for re-engagement with workplace discussion around menopause policy, given that this period has constituted a time when the necessity to engage with workforce diversity[1] has become more essential to organizational survival (Parry and Tochia, 2021). It speculates as to how lockdown could trigger a step-change in attitudes to differential working needs. In doing this, the chapter draws upon a third piece of research by the author on research on work after lockdown (Parry et al, 2021, 2022), which, while not explicitly focused on menopause experiences, in its analysis around diversity management contains organizational learning that has implications for supporting transitions and varied workforce needs.

Starting the conversation about menopause in workplaces

At the root of the challenge of treating menopause as a workforce issue is that it remains a relatively unseen, or marginalized, concern in many organizations. One Head of Diversity and Inclusion in a large organization explained how the non-explicitness of menopause considerations in workforce policy was problematic and prevented useful discussions from progressing that could embed women's needs in HRM practice. The organization's own staff focus groups had revealed that: 'Menopause was coming out as a taboo subject in the workforce. No one wants to talk about menopause, not even women, and it's quite ironic actually that it's probably taken us all this time to bring that "M" word into the workplace.'

This national retail organization was aiming to mainstream menopause discussions, providing a climate where broader aspects of working lives could be openly discussed, such as how employees' confidence and concentration could be affected by the menopause. In practical terms, the organization was facilitating a safe and legitimized space where these discussions could evolve through their Gender Network. They hoped that proactive reflections could feed into this on how employers could support menopause needs.

A representative of another large employer explained that a more staff-focused approach to integrating menopause issues into workforce practice needed to start with ensuring that information and support was accessible, reflecting that policy often failed to resonate with the stakeholders that it was designed to support:

'I think you can have the best policies in the world but if they're not used or touched they will just collect dust and it doesn't have any impact on culture. So actually going out and telling stories and pointing people in the right direction, that is much more useful than saying, "Go and read the policy that we have on menopause", because I think that's really detaching for a colleague.'

Part of a successful approach, this interviewee reflected, was articulating the issues in relatable formats, so that colleagues who were experiencing challenges around the menopause might appreciate the value of making use of organizational resources. One of the ways in which the organization did this was through their staff magazine, which enabled personal stories and support resources to be publicized through the intranet, as well as being directly promoted through their Employee Assistance Programme. Referring to their organization's mental health work, and the synergy it offered for menopause work, the interviewee gave the example of poetry being used on Mental Health Awareness Day to encapsulate issues and stimulate discussion around common, but little-discussed, experiences of working:

> 'So for us telling stories is really important to how we get messages across. So you can get somebody's heart and their head, they will remember that. And even if they don't remember the whole thing, they'll know where to point people to get extra help and support.'

Comparing how momentum had been built around another previously stigmatized workforce group (those experiencing mental health challenges) offers learning potential for organizations. Critically, this organization's approach to legitimizing menopause discussion rested upon a different assumption from the individualized route that employees are more broadly encouraged to take in order to pursue flexible work. Rather, in formulating menopause as a common and collective issue, the intention was that the discussion of workforce solutions would be normalized and access to organizational resources evened out. This represents a conscious effort to heighten the visibility of how the psychological contact can incorporate menopause considerations.

Triggers to engaging with menopause as a workforce issue

One of the issues that came up in the practitioner interviews was that employers tended to be reactive on menopause workplace issues, responding mainly when staffing problems occurred, such as a tribunal bringing organizational deficits into visibility. Aside from their cost implications, tribunals carried the risk of causing lasting reputational damage, stimulating organizations to reflect upon the events that had led them to this point. Conversely, some organizations were taking a longer-term, albeit business-led perspective, studying absence records and retention data and concluding that failing to act on menopause as a workforce issue would damage their efficiency:

'If you look at personnel data and the well-being of women, research that says one in four women consider leaving work because they can't cope with menopause symptoms. Employers know there's a cost of replacing employees and experience.' (Menopause workforce adviser)

Indeed, the same interviewee explained that tapping into a business perspective was proving to be the best way of convincing employers that it was in their interests to take action in developing menopause policy:

'I'll cover off the statistics from how many menopausal women there are in the UK, how many are in work, and if I can get my hands on what their demographics are and what that might mean to them so now and in the future. I'll do stats on: these are the potential number of people, women you're losing due to menopause symptoms. The risk of absence, and the cost of absence, and the cost of tribunals, versus how much it would cost to put it in place, which is quite a simple model, isn't it really?'

In this way, menopause policy was presented neutrally as an investment for human resource management that would rapidly pay off in terms of savings. At present, in order for this information to trigger action around menopause, this trusted third party needed to make a personalized analysis of how action would benefit the employer, a calculation that strategic HRM might be expected to incorporate into its planning processes, but which was currently lacking.

Factors aligned with more listening or proactive employers on menopause workforce policy included having a workforce demographic that offered clear benefits around action, such as a large proportion of older female workers, and personnel factors, including having a sympathetic CEO and board membership. A ripple effect was also observed, in that where leaders were regarded in sectoral communities as 'movers and shakers' then their visible buy-in to menopause policy had positive effects in broadening discussions out to employers who felt that they could be failing to engage with an issue that would give them a competitive edge. On the other hand, a local authority employer reflected, with some surprise, that she regularly sat in meetings discussing workforce issues with other women managers, also of a menopausal age, without the issue of menopause support ever making it onto the agenda.

More broadly, employers' response on the issue was still felt to be lagging and adversarial, representing an impediment to a lasting transformation: 'I think the biggest feedback that I get back, that worries me a little bit, is very often – too often actually, but not every employer says it – somebody will say to me, "Oh we're just giving women another reason to take time off sick"' (Employer support organization).

Achieving cultural shifts around embedded workforce assumptions is a long-term organizational investment. One positive indication that this is in place in some quarters, and will continue to progress, can be taken from employers who were adopting a more proactive approach to menopause, and who were now observing more positive than anticipated staff reactions. A workforce advisor talked about the genuine interest that she observed from male colleagues who were often learning about menopause transitions for the first time. She gave another example of how, when a large organization that they worked with had posted a video on World Menopause Day, it became their most popular social media post of the year, evidence that has the power to convince employers of the value in taking action. She noted that two male managers had been particular advocates of initiating staff discussion around the video, advocating the strong role that leaders and influencers could play in destigmatizing menopause support in the workplace, suggesting that 'it's actually what the trailblazers do that makes the difference'.

Current approaches to menopause as a workforce issue

In both of the research projects drawn upon thus far here, employers were, in large part, dealing with menopause at a broad policy level, collapsing it into occupational health rather than treating it as an employment issue in its own right. This reinforces the idea that menopause requires idiosyncratic responses, rather than moving the agenda forwards in terms of collectivized HRM support that could be mobilized around a predictable part of the work lifecycle. For most of the employers in our research, who were otherwise relatively engaged on age-related workforce issues, there was a lack of explicit engagement with menopause as a workforce issue. To circumvent this obliqueness, one of the projects got at employers' perceptions and practices supporting employees going through the menopause by using a series of vignettes that were presented to employers within the interviews as a spur to reflecting on the kinds of circumstances that might drive a flexible work request and how these might be accommodated. The vignettes depicted four individuals (two men, two women) who were requesting different kinds of flexible working arrangements, enabling employers' responses to both individual circumstances and job design factors to be probed.

One of these vignettes presented an older woman who, while not vocalizing her motivation for applying for a flexible work pattern as stemming from her experience of menopause, was intentionally described as someone who was going through personal discomfort, although it was ambiguous as to whether this would be articulated in her discussions with her manager. Menopause could then be raised in the discussion as a potential drive for more flexible working, and reflected on accordingly. The protagonist was depicted as finding the commute to her place of work increasingly tiring, and as wanting to work from home more often, potentially because her workplace environment was exacerbating her symptoms. She was described as working in an office-based policy job in a local authority, an environment associated with hotdesking and a lack of control over workspace.

Despite the research having been conducted pre-COVID, there was already a great deal of acceptance from employers who were interviewed for the project on the efficiency of working from home. Indeed the predominant assumption was that this kind of working pattern change could be fairly easily informally agreed between line manager and employee without the need to raise a formal request: 'If they're a valued member of staff, and they have value that you're going to struggle to replace in another way, then surely it's in the best interests of the organization to try and accommodate it'. While at first glance, this consensus might seem to provide a supportive climate for employees experiencing the menopause, the reference to initiating individual discussions on a subject that employees are known to be reluctant to raise, with a line manager with whom relationships will vary, adds a dimension of unpredictability to the issue which recourse to a more equitable policy process (that is, a defined menopause policy) may avoid. It was also very common for employers to associate the accommodation of flexible working with employee 'value', suggesting that some employees would be afforded easier access to this route, again evidence of an individualized approach rather than a collective expectation. One suggestion that was made was that in order to broaden access to flexible working, Employee Assistance programmes could play a more active role in 'coaching' employees who felt vulnerable in raising working arrangement issues with their managers in initiating more empowered and less personally risky conversations.

While the majority of employers' responses to the potentially menopause-driven request to work from home vignette centred around a discussion of job tasks and their transferability to the home environment, about a half of respondents drew the conversation back to the context of age and increased tiredness, and referred to organizations' responsibility to conduct an occupational health (OH) assessment to ensure that they were best able to support employees. One interviewee talked about the 'reasonable adjustments' that employers should be making to working practices, reflecting differing health needs within a workforce. If health was identified as a factor, then part-time working was additionally identified by one interviewee as an alternative flexible working strategy to homeworking. The challenge here is whether employees will universally conceptualize their experience of menopause symptoms in health terms, and whether they might be reluctant to do so lest they are regarded as permanently less capable of performing their jobs in previous ways.

One of the problems of collapsing menopause support into occupational health, a relatively common organizational approach, is that, as an employer support organization noted, occupational health practitioners had very often not been brought into this approach. Indeed some were actively antipathetic, regarding menopause as providing a potential increase in their workload. Examples were given in the age-friendly workplaces research (Smeaton and Parry, 2018) of where occupational health teams took a passive approach to involvement in organizational initiatives around menopause and failed to engage in discussion with other stakeholders who were taking up the issue. Transferring responsibility into an area that has already indicated its lack of capacity/suitability represents another way in which employers are attempting to squeeze menopause considerations into existing structures rather than scrutinizing the more fundamental ways in which workforce practice can change to better support a fluctuating set of needs for a significant section of its staff. This is potentially a hurdle to mainstreaming menopause employment policy, and an issue little discussed in the literature.

A solution around conflation with flexible work

The HR manager of a large third sector organization reflected that the potentially daunting process of requesting a flexible working arrangement was complicated by the expectation that it would be initiated through a discussion with one's line manager before it got to the stage of formal application. For some employees, this was precisely the conversation that they were most seeking to avoid, and they were reluctant to personalize this relationship in the way that they felt a discussion of their own health inevitably would:

> 'If you think of a 55/58 year old woman who needs to go and talk to her line manager, who is 30 years old, she's going through the menopause, she's not sleeping at night. She needs to come in at 10 o'clock in the morning because she needs to work like that to help her not be stuffed on a train with everyone around her in … million-degree heat, she needs that. Can you imagine if she had to go and have that conversation with a 30 something year old man who was in financial services, worked 9 to 5, wanted people under his nose, and thought that the woman was just pulling the wool over his eyes?'

Conversely, evidence emerged in the research that some managers were conscious of 'getting it wrong' in their conversations with staff about menopause, a situation that could be exacerbated in organizations that lacked a culture of open discussion around the issue. No evidence emerged in the research of guidance or training for line managers around menopause support, despite the fact that these were organizations otherwise leading on age-friendly good practice, nor still of the kind of equality and diversity training that considered age, gender and menopause, as recommended by Brewis et al's (2017) review of the evidence.

Negative stereotypes around menopause were also felt to mitigate against women raising the issue in the workplace: 'whenever menopause is depicted in the press it's older women in their fifties looking dreadful and women don't associate with that'. Yet menopause is a relatively predictable workforce experience, and flexibility around the location and sequencing of work offers mutual benefits for employees and employers. The lack of evidence that more formalized flexible work policy aligns with menopause considerations for many organizations then represents a missed opportunity in workplace policy.

Employer support organizations were one step ahead here, and tended to regard flexible work as a key resource in managing support needs around the menopause, enabling employees to vary their working hours and place of work around their symptoms and discomfort. It was also noted that, where a more sympathetic climate was promoted around menopause, then managers would be able to have more productive discussions about how work tasks could be varied in a way that promoted organizational efficiency at the same time as it sustained employee well-being. One of the benefits of flexible working arrangements was felt to be that they offered a solution in varying conditions to achieve longer-term staff retention:

'So if somebody is in a job that temporarily is unsuitable for them then maybe we can look at flexible working, you can look at the shift, is there another job that they could do while they come to terms with their menopause symptoms because it doesn't have to be forever?'

Another representative from an employer support organization commented that the need for accommodation around varied well-being could be much shorter term, for example, offering varied working hours to an employee who was having problems sleeping to get through this period, that 'being flexible with flexibility' could be the most suitable support strategy to keep staff in jobs that they otherwise enjoyed, while simultaneously building workforce trust. There are parallels here with what we are seeing in our current research on work during the pandemic, in terms of line managers who understood employees' complicated commitments during lockdown, enabling them to work flexibly, and subsequently seeing enhanced goodwill and productivity (Parry and Tochia, 2021). The necessarily fluctuating pressures which differently regulated lockdowns put on working arrangements may have triggered precisely this kind of agile mindset around job design and its need to be responsive to align with individual circumstances that can also benefit from fresh thinking around menopause workforce support. A cultural shift away from the lock-step expectations of full-time, continuous employment before a cliff-edge retirement (Kojola and Moen, 2016) can be part of a positive shift towards accommodating more diverse workforce needs, with organizations reaping the rewards of cognitive diversity and goodwill around this.

Menopause, workspace and COVID-19

While working from home potentially offers a solution to counter the discomfort of many modern workplaces where people experiencing menopause may, for example, need to manage temperature more effectively, it cannot offer a universal solution for the majority of jobs which cannot be transplanted into the home. As with the working from home issue more broadly, job variation is key in spatial consideration. Office-based jobs offer something of an advantage around menopause management, in that they are both potentially open to redesign in remote or hybrid formats, but also in that they can more easily offer environmental accommodation around menopause, such as the use of fans and better ventilation. Indeed, COVID-19, and potentially also climate change, may have unanticipated effects here, in moving workplace discussions around ventilation forwards more quickly than might otherwise have been the case in the UK. Some indication of where the agenda has thus been accelerated is that in the summer of 2022 the Dutch parliament legislated that employers are required to consider employees' requests to work from home where their work allows it.

However, other working environments, such as production lines, are more fixed and there are fewer opportunities to work from home: evidence that class is an important intersectional factor in women's experience of workforce disadvantage around menopause. Indeed, the interaction of gender and age in employment patterns is important in analysing the benefits of working from home for women's health, since in the UK older workers are more likely to be employed in industries with relatively low levels of working from home (Office for National Statistics, 2021). The professional, scientific and technical sector, which saw the greatest degree of increase in working from home potential during the pandemic (Office for National Statistics, 2021), is also a sector where a minority (6.4 per cent) of older women workers are employed. In contrast, human health and social work, a sector in which a quarter of women in the 'older worker' age group are employed (Office for National Statistics, 2021), was designated a key worker industry during the pandemic, and heavy PPE was essential, a requirement which it might be expected would be challenging for people in menopause who are experiencing hot flushes. Future research might explore how much of a factor menopause is in quitting behaviour in different kinds of jobs, as well as what class dimensions are embedded in this.

Notwithstanding these differences in people in menopause's working experiences, and their varied access to working from home during the pandemic, when we focus on formerly office-based work – which currently represents approximately 45 per cent of jobs (Office for National Statistics, 2021) – it is important to recognize the different ways in which menopause interacts with the change in working location experienced by many in response to successive national lockdowns. While home workspaces offer an environment where autonomy around climate, comfort and work organization can offer obvious physical benefits to people in menopause, so too the pandemic-driven working from home has had consequences around social aspects (Brewis, 2020), which include deficits in the informal connections of the workplace (Parry et al, 2021) and women's increased load of unpaid labour in the emergency circumstances of lockdown (Chung et al, 2021). The latter may have particular significance for women experiencing menopause transitions, given that they are at a life stage likely to overlap with supporting children's online learning or shielding elderly parents, or both simultaneously.

A complicating factor in negotiating new working patterns around menopause is that working from home – the kind of flexible work that might be best suited to promoting physical well-being since staff can control their own environment – was also the format that invoked most distrust from some managers pre-lockdown (Parry, 2017). At the same time there was most buy-in to working from home where managers were more experienced in utilizing it as part of their workforce practice (Parry, 2017). An emerging issue here is whether lockdown and enforced working from home will play to the advantage of menopause management, in that many of these known trust issues have been countered with abundant evidence regarding the productivity of remote workforces under supportive conditions (OECD, 2020; Awarda et al, 2021; Guler et al, 2021). More effective management of menopause symptoms could also be a factor in the reduced absence rates that we saw in our Work after Lockdown research, in that absences that were previously reported as generic sickness that were menopause-related may be easier to cope with at home when employees have greater control over factors like temperature and working hours. At the point of writing, however, it is too early to speculate on the lasting impact of mindset shifts around work organization upon menopause policy and practice, since people in menopause who would prefer to maintain some degree of working from home may also get caught in the backlash around office presence that some organizations are now facing, and these discussions may still be subdued.

Conclusion

There is a danger that when *informal* flexible work is the operational norm that it becomes a perk afforded to higher-status employees who are more easily able to initiate and consolidate these discussions. This can effectively narrow the reach of psychological contracts and muddy the expectations around reciprocal obligations by moving from the idea of collective agreements to individual arrangements. In this context, recognition that significant and valued workforce demographics stand to gain from having the scope to vary their working arrangements around menopause can become lost from the agenda. A further danger associated with informal flexible work is that it takes the onus off managers to design and monitor sustainable flexible working arrangements, transferring this labour onto flexible workers who are expected to make a success of their arrangements lest they inconvenience their employers (Correll et al, 2014; Young, 2018). Managing flexible work may then become yet more invisible labour incorporated by women into their workload, and a double burden at the very time when they were hoping to relieve some of the work-related tensions around menopause, potentially thus setting up more unsustainable working arrangements than if they had been well-supported.

It is essential that the emphasis in flexible work applications moves both from informal to formalized arrangements, and from an expectation of individual initiation to collective right, if it is to acquire the potential to provide support around new ways of working that complement diverse menopause experiences. By explicitly integrating intersectionality into discussions around obligations and needs around menopause, organizations can develop workforce support that more accurately reflects the range and dynamism of experiences around this stage of working lives. Psychological contract fulfilment offers gains for employers as well as employees, since enhanced job satisfaction has been linked to improved productivity

(Karani, Trivedi and Thanki, 2021), so there is a strong impetus for organizations to adopt a more collectivized approach to menopause support embedded in flexible work policy that makes use of the full range of job design possibilities.

There are strong macro, meso and individual level impetuses for delivering enhanced workforce support around menopause. At a societal level, if unsupported menopause experiences are prompting early workforce exit or reduced hours, this can have negative impacts on later life financial well-being, increasing the likelihood of people becoming economically dependent upon families and statutory benefits. At an organizational level, employers may experience increased sick rates and stand to lose some of their most experienced employees, while individually, the comfort, confidence and economic security of people experiencing menopause may be compromised where simple adjustments to working patterns could sustain their participation in jobs.

The pandemic may provide unexpected potential for flexible work to be deployed in a way that better reflects employees' changing working needs around menopause. At the time of writing, many organizations are early in their experimentation with hybrid working models, and key to the success of these will be that managers become skilled at utilizing flexible work *flexibly*, since neither organizations nor employees will want to get tied into contractual change before they have established mutually beneficial working patterns. The pandemic highlighted for managers that their staff were working through a crisis situation amid diverse personal circumstances, and consequently in order to make a success of widespread working from home, it was essential that it be combined with well-managed flexible work that reflected different needs (Parry and Tochia, 2021). The recognition that good, flexible working arrangements should be kept under review and adjusted accordingly is ideally suited to the temporality of menopause experiences.

That said, flexible working may be inaccessible to many people experiencing menopause transitions at work. Women in this age group are more likely to be working in sectors where working from home, and sometimes, too, more varied hours, are a more limited option, such as in healthcare. In the UK, women are also more likely to be in part-time jobs, which employers may already regard as flexible, despite having been designed to reflect organizational rather than individual needs, and thus be unwilling to consider further variation. There remains a challenge to bring the flexible work agenda to the types of work not previously considered in terms of how job design adjustments can enhance employees' motivation, retention and productivity. However, applying flexible work to a broader range of workplace experiences will be essential in extending menopause support across the labour market, and this is particularly urgent where people are working in positions where the characteristics and environments of jobs exacerbate their menopause symptoms. In particular, discussion should extend beyond the white-collar, formerly office-based jobs that have been the focus of much labour theory during the pandemic, in order to better support menopause transitions in lower socio-economic, peripatetic and atypical work. This is essential both on equity grounds, but also in recognition that existing knowledge has concentrated upon the menopause experiences of professional women working in office environments, and to provide a counter to this gap.

Note
[1] An issue that we have looked at in the ESRC project Work After Lockdown: https://www.workafterlockdown.uk/

References

Alcover, C., Rico, R., Turnley, W. and Bolino, M. (2017) 'Understanding the changing nature of psychological contracts in twenty-first century organizations: A multiple-foci exchange relationships approach and proposed framework', *Organizational Psychology Review*, 7(1): 4–35.

Atkinson, C. (2020) 'Flexible working for older workers', in S.H. Norgate and C.L. Cooper (eds) *Flexible Work: Designing Our Healthier Future Lives*, London: Routledge, pp 229–44.

Atkinson, C., Beck, V., Brewis, J., Davis, A. and Duberley, J. (2021) 'Menopause and the workplace: New directions in HRM research and HR practice', *Human Resource Management Journal*, 31(1): 49–64.

Atkinson, C. and Sandiford, P. (2016) 'An exploration of older worker flexibility working arrangements in smaller firms', *Human Resource Management Journal*, 26(1): 12–28.

Awarda, M., Lukas, G., Becerik-Gerber, B. and Roll, S. (2021) 'Working from home during the COVID-19 pandemic: Impact on office worker productivity and work experience', *Work*, 69(4): 1171–89.

Bal, P.M. and Jansen, P.G.W. (2015) 'Idiosyncratic deals for older workers: Increased heterogeneity among older workers enhance the need for i-deals', in Bal, P.M., Kooij, D., and Rousseau, D. (eds) *Aging Workers and the Employer-Employee Relationship*, London: Springer, pp 129–44.

Braun, V. and Clarke, V. (2006) 'Using thematic analysis in psychology', *Qualitative Research in Psychology*, 3 (2): 77–101.

Brewis, J., Beck, V., Davies, A. and Matheson, J. (2017) *The Impact of Menopause Transition on Women's Economic Participation in the UK*, [online] 20 July. Available from: Menopause transition: effects on women's economic participation – GOV.UK (www.gov.uk) [Accessed 17 November 2022].

Brewis, J. (2020) 'The health and socioeconomic impact on menopausal women of working from home', *Case Reports in Women's Health*, 27: e00229. Available from: https://reader.elsevier.com/reader/sd/pii/S221491122 030059X?token=1A6895ABAE2AA0C2C21A493F1602F61D1AF827 4A05B5825D1077A7C1BA2CFC9178C420AAF776AC36D56204152 2E9FEAD&originRegion=eu-west-1&originCreation=20211121160717

Butler, C. (2020) 'Managing the menopause through "abjection work": When boobs can become embarrassingly useful, again', *Work, Employment and Society*, 34(4): 696–712.

Centre for Ageing Better (2020) 'The state of ageing in 2020', [online]. Available from: https://ageing-better.org.uk/sites/default/files/2020-11/ The-State-of-Ageing-2020.pdf [Accessed 27 July 2023].

Chung, H., Birkett, H., Forbes, S. and Seo, H. (2021) 'Covid-19, flexible working and implications for gender inequality in the United Kingdom', *Gender and Society*, 35(2): 218–32.

Cominetti, N. (2021) *A U-Shaped Crisis: The Impact of the COVID-19 Crisis on Older Workers*, Resolution Foundation Briefing, [online]. Available from: https://www.resolutionfoundation.org/app/uploads/2021/04/A-U-shaped-crisis.pdf [Accessed 27 July 2023].

Correll, S.J., Kelly, E.L., O'Connor, T. and Williams, J.C. (2014) 'Redesigning, redefining work', *Work and Occupations*, 41(1): 3–17.

Department for Business, Energy and Industrial Strategy (2021) 'Making flexible working the default', [online]. Available from: https://assets.pub lishing.service.gov.uk/government/uploads/system/uploads/attachme nt_data/file/1019526/flexible-working-consultation.pdf [Accessed 27 July 2023].

Evandrou, M., Falkingham, J., Qin, M. and Vlachantoni, A. (2021) 'Menopausal transition and change in employment: Evidence from the National Child Development Study', *Maturitas*, 143(Jan): 96–104.

Griffiths, A. MacLennan, S.J. and Hassard, J. (2013) 'Menopause and work: An electronic survey of employees' attitudes in the UK', *Maturitas*, 76(2): 155–9.

Guler, M.A., Guler, K., Guneser Gulec, M. and Ozdoglar, E. (2021) 'Working from home during a pandemic', *Journal of Occupational and Environmental Medicine*, 63(9): 731–41.

Hickey, M., Riach, K., Kachouie, R. and Jack, G. (2017) 'No sweat: Managing menopausal symptoms at work', *Journal of Psychosomatic Obstetrics and Gynaecology*, 38(3): 202–9.

Karani, A., Trivedi, P. and Thanki, H. (2021) 'Psychological contract and work outcomes during COVID-19 pandemic', *Journal of Organizational Effectiveness, People and Performance*, 9(1): 149–68.

Kojola, E. and Moen, P. (2016) 'No more lock-step retirement: Boomers' shifting meanings of work and retirement', *Journal of Aging Studies*, 36: 59–70.

Loretto, W. and Vickerstaff, S. (2015) 'Gender, age and flexible working in later life', *Work, Employment and Society*, 29(2): 233–49.

OECD (2020) 'Productivity gains from teleworking in the post-COVID era: How can public policies make it happen?', [online]. Available from: https://www.oecd.org/coronavirus/policy-responses/productivity-gains-from-teleworking-in-the-post-covid-19-era-a5d52e99/ [Accessed 27 July 2023].

Office for National Statistics (2021) 'Living longer: impact of working from home on older workers', [online], 25 August. Available from: https://www.ons.gov.uk/releases/livinglongerimpactofworkingfromhomeonolderworkers [Accessed 27 July 2023].

O'Sullivan, M., Cross, C. and Lavelle, J. (2021) 'Good jobs or bad jobs? Characteristics of older female part-time work', *Industrial Relations*, 52(5): 423–41.

Parry, J. (2017) *Employers, the Right to Request Flexible Working and Older Workers: Research Briefing*, University of Southampton, doi: 10.13140/RG.2.2.11827.84005.

Parry, J., Young, Z., Bevan, S., Veliziotis, M., Baruch, Y., Beigi, M., Bajorek, Z., Salter, E. and Tochia, C. (2021) *Working from Home under COVID-19 lockdown: Transitions and Tensions*, Work After Lockdown, [online]. Available from: https://static1.squarespace.com/static/5f5654b537cea057c500f59e/t/60143f05a2117e3eec3c3243/1611939604505/Wal+Bulletin+1.pdf [Accessed 27 July 2023].

Parry, J., Young, Z., Bevan, S., Veliziotis, M., Baruch, Y., Beigi, M., Bajorek, Z., Richards, S. and Tochia, C. (2022) 'Work after lockdown – No going back: What we have learned working from home through the COVID-19 pandemic', [online]. Available from: https://static1.squarespace.com/static/5f5654b537cea057c500f59e/t/621f392347040c7672afab19/1646213415975/WR_%237379_UoS_WorkAfterLockdownReport_am4_280222_v8.pdf [Accessed 27 July 2023].

Parry, J. and Tochia, C. (2021) 'Diversity management: The need for an intersectional approach in getting at new inequalities prompted by COVID-19 driven working from home', paper presented at the *BSA Work Employment and Society* 2021 virtual conference: Connectedness, Activism and Dignity at Work in a Precarious Era, 25–27 August.

Perlow, L.A. and Kelly, E.L. (2014) 'Toward a module of work redesign for better work and better life', *Work and Occupations*, 41(1): 111–34.

Rousseau, D.M., Ho, V.T. and Greenberg, J. (2006) 'I-Deals: Idiosyncratic terms in employment relationships', *Academy of Management*, 31(4): 977–94.

Smeaton, D. and Parry, J. (2018) *Becoming An Age-friendly Employer: Evidence Report*, Centre for Ageing Better, [online] 10 Sept. Available from: https://www.ageing-better.org.uk/sites/default/files/2018-09/Being-age-friendly-employer-evidence-report.pdf [Accessed 27 July 2023].

Young, Z. (2018) *Women's Work: How Mothers Manage Flexible Working in Careers and Family Life*, Bristol: Bristol University Press.

5

Menopause and Trade Unions

Vanessa Beck

Introduction

This chapter discusses menopause issues in UK workplaces via a lens of trade unions and employment relations. There are four main reasons why a focus on trade unions is important to considerations of menopause in workplaces. The first is the historical role that trade unions have played in the emergent literature on menopause in the workplace. One of the earliest, most comprehensive and still relevant publications (Paul, 2003) was written on behalf of the British Trades Union Congress (TUC). Based on empirical data and providing comprehensive guidance, Paul's publication forms a foundation for much of the subsequent discussions in the field even though very little of this latter discourse was focused on trade unions. Although the early lead in the literature on menopause in work was not pursued by the TUC, they have more recently provided online resources on menopause at work and guidance on supporting women through menopause at work (see www.tuc.org.uk/menopause-work).

Moreover, the TUC and its member unions play an important role in the provision of practical advice and the development of menopause policies and guidelines. This is a second justification for the focus on trade unions. Particularly noteworthy is the Wales TUC Cymru (2017) toolkit for trade unionists on menopause in the workplace, which is not only based on a solid evidence base but also provides clear guidance and comprehensive considerations on how to best introduce a menopause policy or guidelines in a workplace, including deciding which of the two may be most appropriate. Although usually far less comprehensive, many individual trade unions have provided similar advice and guidance, including most of the trade unions represented in the research discussed in this chapter: GMB, Britain's General Union (GMB, nd), National Association of Schoolmasters/Union of Women Teachers (NASUWT, 2021), National Education Union (NEU, 2019), Prospect (2018), Royal College of Nursing (RNC, 2020), University and College Union (UCU, 2018), UNISON, the public sector union (2021) and Unite the Union (Unite, 2012).

Third, and in addition to their work at policy levels, trade unions play a central role in supporting workers in the workplace and are therefore ideally placed to extend this support to include menopause-related issues. It could be questioned whether this support may only be available in unionized workplaces, which might render this point academic in light of the considerable decline in trade union membership (Coderre-LaPalme and Greer, 2018). There are, however, indications that this decline has been halted and potentially even reversed, at least in the public sector (Roper, 2021). Moreover, many trade union campaigns (for example, for a pay rise for key workers, increased rights to flexible working, or decent sick pay for all workers) and support structures (such as those relating to menopause), although primarily aimed at union members, will also benefit individuals irrespective of their union membership and, potentially, their workplace context. The menopause support provided may, in some unions, like Unite (2012), be focussed on the equality and diversity agenda but has elsewhere been incorporated into health and safety or other roles. Our research in this field (see the methodology section) suggests that the latter situation can also result in the inclusion of male allies in menopause discussions as health and safety officers are, at 73 per cent of all individuals holding this role, predominantly male (TUC, 2017).[1]

Relatedly and finally, UK trade unions are also centrally involved in the learning agenda at work (Wallis, Stuart and Greenwood, 2005), for example via TUC Education, and it has become clear that a significant knowledge gap still exists around menopause at work (Atkinson et al, 2021a). Trade unions are again well placed to address this gap, be this in the form of accredited continuous professional development (CPD) for trade union reps and the provision of (online) learning opportunities for all workers (both accessible via www.unionlearn.org.uk), or by lobbying for management training to understand and address issues related to menopause in the workplace. Expressly, this is not about learning to do a job better, and thus enhance productivity – even though it has to be acknowledged that the performance of older workers is often questioned by management – but about learning about menopause experiences in a way that allows everybody in a workplace to understand each other better and improve collegiality and employment relations overall.

These four points form a practical justification for trade unions to play a central role in addressing menopause in workplaces. In addition, this chapter argues for a fifth reason for the involvement of trade unions in these developments, which speaks to the overall trade union ethic of solidarity for the benefit of all workers. It has already been established (Beck, Brewis and Davies, 2020, 2021, and see Atkinson et al in this volume) that significant changes in organizational cultures are required to provide meaningful support to those experiencing menopause transition in workplaces. A common sense of responsibility for well-being at work, understanding of different requirements and preferences of individual workers, and a potentially resulting sense of solidarity in striving for workplaces that provide good working and employment conditions should be part of such organizational change. It is in this area that the underlying principles of the trade union movement, a joining together of members to protect themselves and advance workers' interests, is essential. And although Morgan and Pulignano (2020) outline an overall decline in workplace solidarity, they also point to remaining levels of traditional as well as newly emerging forms of solidarity at work. Within trade union activities, as among other collective groups of employees, there is thus not only a focus on collective action, such as in strikes, but also concern with shared material contexts, institutional frameworks of laws and regulations. All of these might bond workers and their social communities but these arenas are equally relevant for individuals experiencing menopause while at work.

According to a position statement by the European Menopause and Andropause Society (Rees et al, 2021) workplaces should create open, inclusive and supportive cultures involving, where possible, collaboration between occupational health professionals and HR managers. As the authors say: 'Women should not be discriminated against, marginalized or dismissed because of menopausal symptoms' (Rees et al, 2021, p 56). Trade unions and professional associations are specifically mentioned as possible sources of help and advice when workplace needs go unacknowledged or are not supported. Collective action in workplaces and support for individuals is thus a clear objective in improving the situation for those experiencing menopause transition at work. This is especially important given the traditional focus of trade unions on working class occupations and workplaces as Delanoe et al (2012) show that lower-class women tend to experience more severe menopause symptoms within and across different countries and ethnic groups. Class can thus be an important social context for menopause experiences.

Yoeli, Macnaughton and McLusky (2021) confirm this assessment with their work on casual, informal and precarious jobs. They also find that individuals in lower-paid and more manual jobs are more likely to experience a higher number of psychosocial menopause symptoms than white collar female workers. Interestingly, however, Yoeli et al also highlight the importance of broader life circumstances, including gendered disadvantage, poverty and intersectional marginalization, as influential on menopause symptoms and experiences, thus reflecting the shared material contexts in which workers and communities might bond and provide mutual solidarity (Morgan and Pulignano, 2020). Most significantly, though, it is pointed out that menopausal women in casualized and marginalized jobs are least likely to benefit from 'recommendations, innovations or protections of the "menopause at work" policies introduced by organisations or trade unions' (Yoeli, Macnaughton and McLusky, 2021, p 20), thus making attention to differences in the workforce by trade unions essential. However, this is not to negate the often silenced, shameful and stigmatized experience of menopause at work for the majority of women in the UK where it is 'neither ritualized nor associated with socially recognized status change' (de Salis et al, 2018, p 535).

Even more, trade unions often campaign for broader social benefits and values (Valentini et al, 2020) and it is here that there is considerable opportunity for unions to not only address menopause as an issue affecting up to half of the population (Grandey, Gabriel and King, 2020) but also to benefit the workforce as a whole. This dual approach to a specific issue and broader social workforce engagement could be an important strategy of (continued) trade union renewal. In light of unions' recent and rather turbulent developments, a focus on majoritarian views and a rejection of narrow, self-serving issues have been found to be important union strategies (for example, for the RMT, see Valentini et al, 2020). Connolly (2020) similarly discusses democratic processes involving union officials and activists as a means for union renewal, especially where their work is being compromised by the challenges of austerity measures.

This chapter therefore seeks to make two contributions. On the one hand, it is argued that engagement with the taboo subject of the menopause in the public media and in workplaces might be part of a useful trade union renewal strategy. On the other hand, the chapter shows how, by responding to the need for support among those experiencing menopause transitions while in work, trade unions can also enhance employment and working conditions for workforces at large. The two arguments are co-dependent in that increasing social awareness of menopause and of trade union activity in this field would make for greater union leverage to ensure broader workplace change. In addition, both sit within a broader understanding of employment relations and collegiality which benefits from solidarity among and between workforces. This broader focus is not intended to detract from the important focus on the experience of menopause transition. For many this is a difficult, challenging time and being heard and seen in this situation is vital. However, the broader focus taken in this chapter suggests ways in which such attention could be achieved from a broader range of individuals who might, as a result, be better placed to provide support or at least understanding for those transitioning through menopause.

In the following, the experiences of menopause in workplaces will be outlined to highlight the role of unions. Following this, the methods employed in the empirical investigations that this chapter reports on will be provided. Empirical material will then be presented to show both how trade union work addresses menopause taboos and issues, and how this can be utilized to enhance employment and working conditions. Finally, conclusions will be drawn for how trade unions could take menopause in workplaces forward in a way that might also benefit the trade union movement itself.

Menopause in the workplace: a trade union issue

There is a significant evidence base on issues related to menopause in the workplace, although a fair amount of it has been published in the popular press, in grey literature and online, which can make obtaining reliable and consistent information difficult. This is at least in part due to the magnitude of the issue with Papadatou (2019), for example, suggesting that across the UK workforce a potential 14 million working days per year are lost due to women having to take time out to alleviate menopause symptoms. Since our Government Equalities Office report on the interrelationship between menopause experiences and economic participation in the UK (Brewis et al, 2017), a literature focussed on workplace contexts from both a sociology of work and employment as well as an organizational and human resources perspective has emerged. This also includes a trade union literature that tends to take a more practical and policy-oriented approach. This literature has been found to be reliable and essential for employers to read and act upon by Jack et al (2014, 2016) who especially highlight the consistent guidance provided by Paul (2003) on behalf of the TUC. The importance of Paul's report has already been outlined. To reiterate: this means that trade unions have a well-established and significant contribution to addressing menopause in the workplace.

Based on Paul (2003) and with progress made since then (Hardy, Hunter and Griffiths, 2018), trade unions have provided evidence on and further reinforced our understanding of the relationship between menopause and the workplace as a bi-directional one. There is significant information on the range of menopause symptoms that have an impact on how work is undertaken, with questions being raised as to whether this also affects individuals' performance at work (Beck et al, 2021). In turn, workplaces can have detrimental effects on individuals experiencing menopause transitions with, for example, 22 per cent of Paul's (2003) respondents identifying work as making symptoms such as hot flushes, tiredness, sweating and mood swings, among others, worse. Although there are weaknesses in the methodology Paul employed and her findings are now somewhat dated, other literature (Atkinson et al, 2021a; Steffan, 2021; van der Heijden, Pak and Santana, 2021) reinforces this overall image of a two-way relationship.

The previously discussed aim to provide a culture of support can be used as an example to explore the role of trade unions in concrete terms and demonstrate why menopause at work is a trade union issue. A decisive factor determining whether support that might be available can be accessed is the issue of disclosure. Studies have reported varying levels of menopause status disclosure in workplaces but rarely suggest that more than 50 per cent of women have disclosed (Brewis et al, 2017). The time where this makes a real difference is when menopause symptoms result in sickness absence (Geukes et al, 2020). And Hardy et al (2018) report (allowable) sickness absence (for example to attend a medical appointment) being mentioned frequently in employers' policies on menopause. Yet a survey conducted by the National Union of Teachers showed that while 20 per cent of their respondents had taken sick leave as a result of menopause symptoms, over 80 per cent did not give their manager the real reason for their absence (Chartered Institute of Personnel and Development, 2019). This seems to suggest that a good intention to provide support might exist in some workplaces but that a culture of not talking about menopause at work hinders women from accessing such support.

The reasons behind women's reluctance to disclose their menopause status show the importance of trade union activities in these areas. Embarrassment or seeing menopause as a private issue apart, there are suggestions that those experiencing menopause transition are concerned about being perceived negatively or that their abilities would be questioned (Beck, Brewis and Davies, 2020). This speaks of insecurities in relation to job status, and potentially of concerns about performance management and job loss (Beck, Brewis and Davies, 2021). There are two ways in which these issues can be addressed. On the one hand, there are numerous recommendations to increase staff awareness and challenge negative stereotypes (Griffiths, MacLennan and Hassard, 2013, 2016; Jack et al, 2014; Paul, 2003) to reduce the stigma and taboo in talking about menopause at work. While this is undoubtedly an aim, such development is likely to only be achievable in the long-term. Moreover, it still requires individuals experiencing menopause to disclose with the potential side-effect of feeling vulnerable and exposed.

A possible alternative is therefore to pursue key trade union strategies, such as the enhanced right to flexible working, decent sick pay and absence policies (see inter alia TUC, 2022). These can be implemented without having to identify specific, let alone 'qualifying' menopause symptoms that would entitle the person suffering from such symptoms to access workplace adjustments. More comprehensive employment and working conditions would support all workers and would negate the need to disclose, while at the same time accommodating requirements as necessitated by menopause symptoms. These might include the need to start some working days later due to night sweats or insomnia as well as to take time off for medical appointments and/or due to temporarily severe symptoms, including heavy bleeding or migraines. Trade union demands and strategies that are already being pursued (see for example some of the activities discussed later in this chapter) are thus a useful way to consider how menopause at work can be addressed. As a number of trade union website and reports (see for example UNISON, 2021; Prospect, 2018) thus make explicit, menopause is a workplace issue and therefore also a trade union issue.

The following section outlines the research on which this chapter is based. Subsequently, the possibilities for an interrelationship between tackling the menopause taboo, enhancing support for individuals experiencing menopause, better employment and working conditions, and trade union renewal strategies are outlined, and the relevance of embedding menopause support in enhanced employment and working conditions for workforces at large is discussed.

Methodology

The research for this chapter is made up of a number of projects and stages as outlined in what follows. Although not all of the individual elements of this research are explicitly drawn upon in the data that are presented and analysed, they jointly form a comprehensive and solid evidence base. The first project was undertaken by the editors of this book in collaboration with Andrea Davies and TUC Education and was funded by an Economic and Social Research Council (ESRC) Impact Acceleration Account (IAA) grant from the University of Bristol. There were three stages to this project: an online, baseline survey, 11 workshops with trade union representatives in ten UK cities and a follow-up survey with workshop participants.

A link to the baseline online survey was circulated via TUC Education networks, social media, academic mailing lists and personal networks. The survey was designed to encompass a range of issues pertaining to menopause in the workplace and covered background characteristics; employment and working conditions; menopause information, guidance or policies in the workplace; and knowledge and perceptions about menopause in general and in the workplace. There were opportunities throughout and at the end of the survey to add further qualitative information. The survey was open from 7 June 2018 to 26 July 2018 and was completed by 5,417 individuals, of which 5,399 responses could be used for analysis. This survey, and the strengths and weaknesses of the dataset, have been reported on previously (see Beck, Brewis and Davies, 2020). The data gathered are also analysed in Chapter 6 by Jo Brewis.

In the second stage, intensive action research at 11 workshops was undertaken between 6 September 2018 and 29 November 2018. The workshops were held in ten UK cities and attended by 139 trade union representatives in total, representing nine industries across the public, private and third sectors. They were designed as CPD events for trade union representatives with the intention to provide them with knowledge and information that they would be able to use in their respective workplaces. At the same time, the innovative action research approach ensured discussion of issues and problems in providing menopause support in workplaces, and the development of practical solutions, alongside the collection of research data.

Following on from these workshops, all participants were invited to complete a survey which was an adjusted version of the initial survey. The follow-up survey ran from 12 March to 19 April 2019 and 37 workshop participants responded. As in the initial survey, there were ample opportunities for qualitative feedback as part of this survey. This dataset has not previously been analysed independently. It forms an important aspect of this chapter as it is an overview of trade union representatives' engagement with workplaces regarding menopause.

After the ESRC IAA project ended, two further research projects were undertaken that allowed for an extension of the investigation. As part of the workshops delivered in collaboration with TUC Education, participants were not only asked to take part in the follow-up survey outlined in the previous paragraph but also whether they would be willing to be interviewed further down the line. At the University of Bristol, funding from the Department of Management's General Research Fund allowed for these interviews to be undertaken and transcribed. Interviews with 27 workshop participants were conducted between 1 February 2019 and 31 July 2019.

Finally, a contact established at one of the workshops undertaken with TUC Education led to further, unfunded research being undertaken in a local council. The author remained in contact with a UNISON and a Unite representative who had introduced menopause support structures into their workplace. Contact was established in October 2018 and has been maintained since to research these support structures. Two surveys of council staff were undertaken, the first one between 17 May 2019 and 21 December 2019 (to capture as broad a range of responses as possible) and the second between 15 January 2021 and 31 March 2021 to establish longer-term trends.

For all projects reported on here we have to assume that self-selection into participation resulted in a sample bias towards individuals interested in, experiencing or knowledgeable about menopause. Commensurately, the results indicate a high degree of awareness and knowledge about menopause. The next section outlines some key characteristics of the trade unions represented in our research, as well as background information on our respondents.

The diversity of trade union contexts

In the initial baseline survey, a drop-down menu of 52 unions was provided with additional options being 'no union membership' and 'other': 157 respondents provided further details on other trade unions that they were members of, including specialist trade unions, professional bodies and international trade unions. As is visible in Figure 5.1, the largest group of respondents at 37.3 per cent were not members of a trade union. However, when combining all unions, membership exceeded non-membership. This may be the result of the research being undertaken in collaboration with trade unions but could also be an indication of the continued importance of trade unions across workplaces. The data presented have been recoded to combine all other union membership and focus on those unions for whom there are meaningful data. Even with this recoding, some of the unions with fewer respondents (for example NEU, Chartered Society of Physiotherapy (CSP), Prospect and GMB) cannot be further differentiated without opening up the possibility that individuals could be identifiable. The union membership of respondents in the follow-on survey of workshop participants shows a similar pattern, with UNISON being represented most. The distribution varies somewhat from the baseline survey as all attendees at workshops and therefore all respondents to the post-workshop survey were union members by definition.

The data available allow us an insight into the attitudes and experiences concerning menopause in a diverse range of unions, sectors and occupations (Table 5.1). For contextualization, the following table provides an overview of the size and focus of the unions for whom both surveys provide meaningful data, that is UNISON,

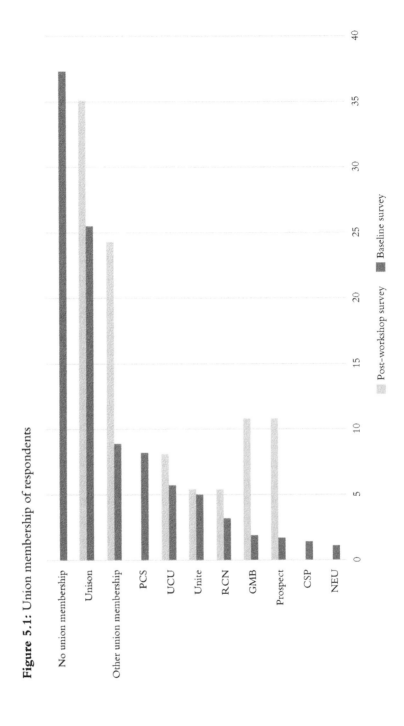

Figure 5.1: Union membership of respondents

Table 5.1: Overview of trade unions' size and focus

	Membership 2013–14	Current membership (websites)	Focus
UNISON (www.unison.org.uk)	1,283,000	1.3 million	Public services and utilities, in public and private sectors
UCU (University and College Union, www.ucu.org.uk)	106,000	130,000	Staff in universities, colleges, prisons, adult education and training organizations
Unite (www.unitetheunion.org)	1,405,000	1.4 million	Construction, manufacturing, transport, logistics
RCN (Royal College of Nursing, Union and professional body, www.rcn.org.uk)	422,000	465,000	Nurses, midwives, health care assistants, nursing associates and students
GMB (Britain's General Union, www.gmb.org.uk)	617,000	600,000	Retail, security, schools, distribution, the utilities, social care, the NHS, ambulance service and local government
Prospect (https://prospect.org.uk)	116,000	145,000	Engineers, managers, scientists and other specialists in public and private sectors

UCU, Unite, RCN, GMB and Prospect. The comparison with historical membership data based on information from Coderre-LaPalme and Greer (2018) for 2013–14 shows stability in membership (UNISON, Unite) and some indications of moderate membership growth (UCU, RCN, Prospect). Only the GMB figures suggest a small contraction although all figures here are indicative and not too much should be read into them.

Most respondents and interviewees, their trade union membership aside, were female, though there were, in the initial baseline survey, 7.7 per cent of respondents who identified as a man and there were six men who took part in the workshops. There was one man who completed the post-workshop survey but no men were interviewed in the follow-up research. With the focus of the research being on menopause, the gender divide of respondents is not a surprise. Given the small numbers of men in these categories, results are not broken down by gender and union to avoid accidental identification.

Respondents were also asked about their ethnicity. Although the majority of respondents in each union are white, there were significant numbers of Black/African/Caribbean/Black British respondents in Unite, and of Mixed/multiple ethnic groups respondents in UCU and Prospect. There are some questions about the accuracy of this data, though, as there were also significant numbers who preferred not to provide information on their ethnicity (for example members of Prospect). In parallel with issues around disclosure of menopause, if this were due to respondent concerns about the implications of revealing their ethnicity, then this is worrying in itself. In addition, this highlights two problematic issues. The first is that very little is known about the differences in how menopause is experienced at work according to ethnicity and background (Atkinson et al, 2021a). Anecdotal information from our research shows, for example, that for some groups the use of the term 'menopause' alone is a sufficient barrier to engagement and might mean that they do not engage with discussions and support around menopause at all. A much better understanding of such differences is required to ensure that appropriate support can be provided for each group. A second problem is that the preference to not provide information on ethnicity could be an indicator of racist or other discriminatory experiences (Targett and Beck, 2022) and could mean that, for individuals already struggling with other issues, association with menopause is a factor too far, again potentially resulting in insufficient or inappropriate support or lack of access to such support that may be accessible for other groups.

As these background data already indicate, the issues surrounding menopause in the workplace will not be the same in all unions and there are limitations to what our data allow us to investigate, in particular in relation to gender and ethnicity. The sectors and occupations covered by a union (for example if we compare office work, nursing, teaching or retail work) all bring their own challenges, as does the makeup of the workforce in terms of gender, age and ethnicity. It is not possible to cover all of these in any depth so this chapter, alongside a general overview, will therefore highlight some challenges and provision of support in specific circumstances as well as raising the need for further work in these areas. As already indicated, identification of statements associated with and positions within particular unions, sectors or locations is avoided to ensure anonymity.

Trade union discussions and activities to break the taboo

There are plenty of examples to show that menopause in the workplace remains a taboo subject matter to which additional attention needs to be paid (Hardy et al, 2019; Beck, Brewis and Davies, 2020; Atkinson et al, 2021b). Our evidence shows that trade unions have started engaging in conversations around menopause that help to address this taboo, even if overcoming it still seems a rather distant possibility. For example, one respondent to the follow-up survey answered the question 'Has change occurred as a result of action taken following the workshop?' by stating that 'more women have come to us and more are willing to engage and share experiences'. Similarly, interviews with workshop attendees showed that their increased level of knowledge and, potentially, self-confidence in talking about menopause in work-based conversations allowed the subject matter to emerge in conversations about other problems:

'Lots of people come to me about one thing and end up talking to me about something else. So, they might come to me because, I don't know, they're struggling with sickness absence or someone at work at the moment who I'm supporting, off and on, who said to me she was struggling with too much work. There were two colleagues, and they were in a new job and she said "I don't know if this is the job for me and actually there's just so much work", they were both saying "there's just so much work, we're really struggling with it". They were both in their forties and they were both saying the same thing, and I did believe it was the case that the work they were doing, there was just too much of it. But, what usually happens is I get this and then someone, on a one to one, will confide about other things that are going on in their life. And this one lady [of the two colleagues mentioned before], she was talking about the menopause, she was perimenopaus[al], and she was saying "I'm really struggling with the hot flushes and things".'

When we compare the baseline survey, which includes non-union members, with the post-workshop survey (union members only), there are thus subtle differences in that the latter are more likely to consider menopause to be something that can be discussed at work, though part of this effect might be as a result of greater exposure to menopause issues as part of the workshops and beyond. These data are represented in Figure 5.2.

A further question was asked in both surveys to establish what kind of conversations individuals were having about menopause in the workplace. As Figure 5.3 shows, there are indications that perhaps more conversations were taking place overall following the workshops as there were more experiences of both a positive and a negative nature. Our post-workshop data also suggest that there were fewer conversations being held only among women. It is noteworthy that this was a multi-answer question, so responses are not necessarily mutually exclusive.

The almost 30 per cent of post-workshop respondents who indicated 'other' conversations were asked to provide further information on the nature of these experiences of talking about menopause with other people at work. Half of these respondents mentioned having spoken to management in their capacity as trade union representatives. One respondent thus stated: 'As a shop steward I have raised the menopause in meetings amongst senior managers who are male and they have been sympathetic'. Additional comments here included trade union representatives supporting staff members either via conversations or in performance management procedures, within the union, and to develop a policy on menopause in the workplace. One respondent mentioned that the experience of talking about menopause issues had been 'unnecessarily difficult' and another stated that while they were happy to talk about it, others were embarrassed by the subject matter. Our data thus suggest that while trade union representatives are not a solution to problems of menopause being a taboo as a whole, they are able to increase conversations about menopause in the workplace and to do this in a way that can help individual employees as well as managers.

In addition to qualitative responses to our two surveys and follow-up interviews showing how a union context is an important location for discussions on menopause in workplaces, further empirical results suggest that menopause could become a useful strategy for trade union renewal. During the workshops, possible actions were discussed and so workshop participants were asked which ideas they planned to tackle as part of the post-workshop survey. The level of activity and engagement that our results suggest is significant, as displayed in Figure 5.4.

The follow-up interviews also showed that there was a general drive towards information provision and that this was happening in two directions. First, individuals who had attended a workshop were using

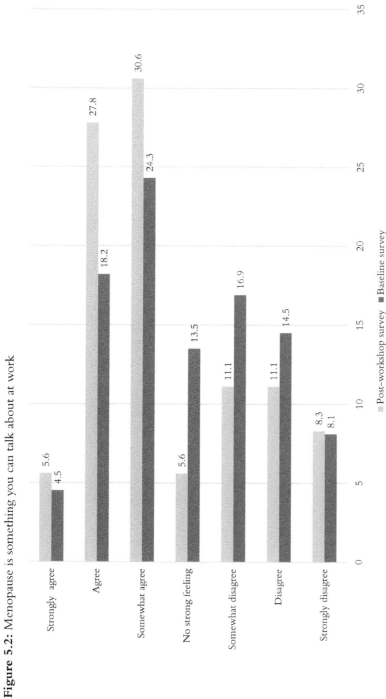

Figure 5.2: Menopause is something you can talk about at work

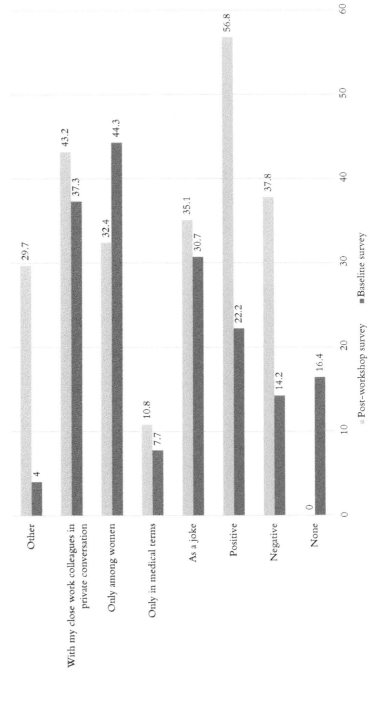

Figure 5.3: What is your experience of talking about the menopause with other people at work?

their knowledge to inform their unions, where background knowledge on menopause and how to approach it was often 'a little behind' as one respondent suggested. In the following interview excerpt, this respondent talks about implementing a workplace menopause policy as well as becoming involved in their union's work via their Equality Conference.

Interviewer: Which action have you taken following participation in the workshop?

Interviewee: I have tabled the [name of organization] policy at our H&S committee and as a first step it will be going on our staff well-being site. I have insisted that it is set in policy as well longer term and suggested it would be a positive in recruitment. I attended the [union] Equality Conference and attended the menopause workshop. I think I knew more from the TUC day than those running the [union] session. [Name of union] were on the brink of releasing guidance and acknowledged that they are a little behind with this.

In addition to these union and workplace level activities, interviews revealed the level of demand within workplaces for information on menopause. This meant that activists and union reps also required more information to allow them to help individual members:

'And one thing that kept coming back through our women's conference and our evaluation forms was they wanted more information on the menopause. And then the other side of that, and it's something I'm working on at the moment, is our activists were also … because it's something that it has been raising its … raising itself in the workplace sort of, you know, the last, I don't know, three to five years, our activists wanted advice on how to help members who they felt were suffering with the menopause in work and how best to help them.'

Trade union representatives who are interested in and knowledgeable about menopause were thus driving unions' agendas as well as providing support and advice to individuals. There was also a sense of not simply helping union members who were experiencing menopause while at work. Many of the representatives were themselves menopausal and thus had a personal interest in finding solutions to problematic menopause symptoms. As the following extract from one of the follow-up interviews suggests, it seemed that the stars were aligning between the representative's own experience of menopause, social and other media attention to menopause, and employers becoming aware that they needed to take action on menopause issues:

'Yeah, I mean … it's … a few of those things are … it's … working from a trade union and a very female-dominated trade union, obviously health issues that affect women have always been, kind of, a big part of what we kind of look at and campaign around. And obviously, with, you know, going through the menopause myself, kind of, the two came together. It also appeared kind of, a bit more in the media and in … kind of … being discussed. Do you know what I mean? Kind of progressive employers were, you know, taking the issue on and doing something about it. So it just … it just seemed kind of, the time to actually get my own employer to do something about it.'

The support provided via trade union representatives thus extends beyond trade union members and includes, as demonstrated in the 'action plans' in Figure 5.4, the workforce as a whole (for example restrooms, quiet space, gender inclusivity, water coolers, and so on), management's ability to work with their staff teams (for example via training, policies, and so on), the health and safety agenda (risk assessments) and well-being agenda. The overall approach to talking about menopause and increasing as well as enhancing workplace communication could also be seen as a benefit to overall employment relations. Such a broad agenda for action might also allow the development of a strategy that overcomes Yoeli, Macnaughton and McLusky (2021, p 20) critique that '[m]enopausal women in casual jobs will likely not benefit from the recommendations, innovations or protections of the "menopause at work" policies introduced by organisations or trade unions'.

In looking ahead to how such a progressive position taken by trade unions might influence their overall position and attractiveness to a much broader section of the workforce, the next quotation indicates how efforts to introduce a workplace statement of intent on menopause led to recruiting new union members:

'OK, so what we did was, we had quite a structured couple of meetings, so myself and a couple of other reps. We produced some

Figure 5.4: Post-workshop menopause action plans

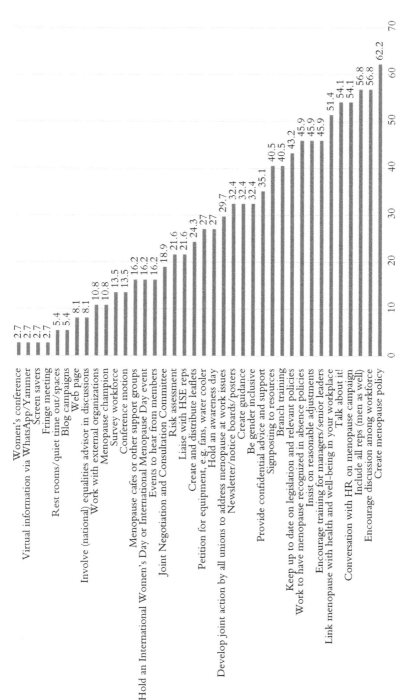

posters, we asked for a ... we produced a questionnaire that we sent out to our members, and anybody else actually that wanted to fill it in, and we, on the back of that in actual fact got new members to [name of] union as well, and I got a lot of good reports.'

Conclusion

This chapter began with a discussion of the importance of trade unions in the process of attending to menopause issues in workplaces and also outlined the foundational work that unions have undertaken in contributing to both the literature in the field and the practice in workplaces. This practice has included an important role in developing policies and guidelines, offering practical support to individuals in workplaces, and trade unions' contribution to the learning agenda in supporting development opportunities and the building of a knowledge base about menopause at work.

Trade unions have thus been an important force in helping to break the taboo that exists around menopause conversations in workplaces. As the empirical data has shown, this is at least in part due to broader social discussions on menopause, including celebrity engagement such as the Davina McCall documentaries and policy developments including the lobbying by the All-Party Parliamentary Group on menopause and the appointment of a hormone replacement therapy tsar to ensure supply. Unions have thus benefitted from a general groundswell of attention to menopause. However, they have contributed significantly on specific aspects, in particular in pressurizing management and employers to up their game and in providing support to individuals (usually members). Although they are therefore important players in tackling the menopause taboo, it tends to be their members only who benefit from such one-to-one support. As Riach and Jack (2021) point out, employees who have (easier) access to trade union membership are also likely to be more securely employed, and it is therefore important to consider different levels of insecurity and precarity in a broad range of workplaces. To investigate to what extent this might be possible, this chapter considered trade unions' activities in relation to menopause in light of the impact on the overall workforce's employment and working conditions.

Indeed, much of the work that is being undertaken by trade unions in this field will benefit employees irrespective of their trade union membership. Broader union advocacy on flexibility, sick pay or absence policies would be likely to make a difference across the workforce as a whole. The same would be true of infrastructure changes in relation to temperature control, access to water and to appropriate sanitary facilities, including showers, as these would be available to all workers. It is not as straightforward to make a case that the recent attention to menopause policies or guidelines would lead to improvements for the whole workforce. And yet there are organizations in which such policies or guidelines have been integrated into either equality policies and guidelines or into the health and safety agenda. If such a move can be accompanied by a general strengthening of either of these approaches, then broader benefits are conceivable. This is especially the case if a parallel benefit is better knowledge and understanding about menopause across the workforce as this would allow for mutual support and, potentially, wider conversations about menopause. This might mean broader support for individuals that does not rely purely on individual union representatives but could also be provided by colleagues, managers, and occupational health. Thus, this chapter sought to demonstrate that, via support already being provided to those experiencing menopause transitions while in work, trade unions can enhance employment and working conditions for workforces as a whole.

In return, unions' involvement in such a range of activities would add a further string to their bow of employment and broader social relevance. The media and policy attention being paid to menopause shows how significant an issue this is for, as keeps being pointed out, at least half the population. Riding on the crest of this wave of attention would aid unions in their bid to regain and maintain a powerful and well-supported position. And as this chapter has shown from the start, unions have a historically grounded right to be involved in, if not lead on, these discussions given their long-term contributions and innovations in the field. Although somewhat far-fetched overall, though, as our empirical data show, definitely true in certain circumstances, trade unions' involvement with the menopause agenda can be a part of their renewal strategy.

Note

[1] Male allyship at work is also discussed in Chapter 7 by Hannah Bardett, Kathleen Riach and Gavin Jack.

References

Atkinson, C., Beck, V., Brewis, J., Davies, A. and Duberley, J. (2021a) 'Menopause and the workplace: New directions in HRM research and HR practice', *Human Resource Management Journal*, 31(1): 49–64.

Atkinson, C., Carmichael, F. and Duberley, J. (2021b) 'The menopause taboo at work: Examining women's embodied experiences of menopause in the UK police service', *Work, Employment and Society*, 35(4): 657–76.

Beck, V., Brewis, J. and Davies, A. (2020) 'The remains of the taboo: Experiences, attitudes and knowledge about menopause in the workplace', *Climacteric*, 23(2): 158–64.

Beck, V., Brewis, J. and Davies, A. (2021) 'Women's experience of menopause at work and performance management', *Organization*, 23(3): 510–20.

Brewis, J., Beck, V., Davies, A. and Matheson, J. (2017) *The Impact of Menopause Transition on Women's Economic Participation in the UK*, [online] 20 July, Available from: https://www.gov.uk/government/publications/menopause-transition-effects-on-womens-economic-participation [Accessed 17 November 2022].

Chartered Institute of Personnel and Development (2019) 'The menopause at work. A guide for people professionals', [online] 9 August, Available from: https://www.cipd.org/en/knowledge/guides/menopause-people-professionals-guidance/ [Accessed 27 July 2023].

Coderre-LaPalme, G. and Greer, I. (2018) 'Dependence on a hostile state: UK trade unions before and after Brexit', in Lehndorff, S., Dribbusch, H. and Schulten, T. (eds) *Rough Waters. European Trade Unions in a Time of Crisis*, Brussels: ETUI, pp 259–84.

Connolly, H. (2020) '"We just get a bit set in our ways": Renewing democracy and solidarity in UK trade unions', *Transfer*, 26(2): 207–22.

Delanoe, D., Hajri, S., Bachelot, A., Draoui, D., Hassoun, D., Marsican, E. and Ringa, V. (2012) 'Class, gender and culture in the experience of menopause: A comparative survey in Tunisia and France', *Social Science & Medicine*, 75(2): 401–9.

De Salis, I., Owen-Smith, A., Donovan, J. and Lawlor, D. (2018) 'Experiencing menopause in the UK: The interrelated narratives of normality, distress, and transformation', *Journal of Women & Aging*, 30(6): 520–40.

Geukes, M., Oosterhof, H., van Aalst, M. and Anema, J. (2020) 'Attitude, confidence and social norm [sic] of Dutch occupational physicians regarding menopause in a work context', *Maturitas*, 139: 27–32.

GMB (nd) 'Smash the stigma: Menopause in the workplace', [online], Available from: http://www.gmb.org.uk/menopause [Accessed 28 June 2022].

Grandey, A.A., Gabriel, A.S. and King, E. (2020) 'Tackling taboo topics: A review of the three Ms in working women's lives', *Journal of Management*, 46(1): 7–35.

Griffiths, A., MacLennan, S.J. and Hassard, J. (2013) 'Menopause and work: An electronic survey of employees' attitudes in the UK', *Maturitas*, 76(2): 155–59.

Griffiths, A., Ceausu, I., Depypere, H., Lambrinoudaki, I., Mueck, A., Pérez-López, F., van der Schouw, Y., Senturk, L., Simoncini, T., Stevenson, J., Stute, P. and Rees, M. (2016) 'EMAS recommendations for conditions in the workplace for menopausal women', *Maturitas*, 85(1): 79–81.

Hardy, C., Hunter, M. and Griffiths, A. (2018) 'Menopause and work: An overview of UK guidance', *Occupational Medicine*, 68(9): 580–6.

Hardy, C., Griffiths, A., Thorne, E. and Hunter, M. (2019) 'Tackling the taboo: Talking menopause-related problems at work', *International Journal of Workplace Health Management*, 12(1): 28–38.

Jack, G., Pitts, M., Riach, K., Bariola, E., Schapper, J. and Sarrel, P. (2014) 'Women, work and the menopause: Releasing the potential of older professional women', [online], final project report, La Trobe University, Melbourne, Australia, Available from: https://womenworkandthemenopa use.com/final-project-pdf-download/ [Accessed 4 April 2022].

Jack, G., Riach, K., Bariola, E., Pitts, M., Schapper, J. and Sarrel, P. (2016) 'Menopause in the workplace: What employers should be doing', *Maturitas*, 85: 88–95.

Morgan, G. and Pulignano, V. (2020) 'Solidarity at work: Concepts, levels and challenges', *Work, Employment and Society*, 34(1): 18–34.

NASUWT (2021) 'Managing the menopause in the workplace', [online], Available from: www.nasuwt.org.uk/advice/equalities/under-represen ted-groups/women/managing-the-menopause-in-the-workplace.html [Accessed 28 June 2022].

National Education Union (2019) 'Menopause', [online], Available from: https://neu.org.uk/menopause [Accessed 28 June 2022].

Papadatou, A. (2019) 'Menopause costs UK economy 14 million working days per year', *HR Review*, [online], Available from: www.hrreview.co.uk/ hr-news/menopause-costs-uk-economy-14-million-working-days-per-year/115754 [Accessed 28 June 2022].

Paul, J. (2003) 'Working through the change: Health and safety and the menopause', report for the Trades Union Congress, [online] March, Available from: https://www.hazards.org/haz82/menopause.pdf [Accessed 27 July 2023].

Prospect (2018) 'A members' guide to the menopause: A workplace issue', [online], Prospect, Available from: https://library.prospect.org.uk/down load/2018/02067 [Accessed 28 June 2022].

Royal College of Nurses (2020) 'Menopause: RCN guidance for nurses, midwives and health visitors', [online], Available from: www.rcn.org. uk/professional-development/publications/rcn-menopause-guidance-for-nurses-midwives-and-health-visitors-uk-pub-0093326 [Accessed 28 June 2022].

Rees, M., Bitzer, J., Cano, A., Ceausu, I., Chedraui, P., Durmusoglu, F. et al (2021) 'Global consensus recommendations on menopause in the workplace: A European Menopause and Andropause Society (EMAS) position statement', *Maturitas*, 151: 55–62.

Riach, K. and Jack, G. (2021) 'Women's health in/and work: Menopause as an intersectional experience', *International Journal of Environmental Research and Public Health*, 18(20): 10793.

Roper, C. (2021) 'Good news, bad news and the same challenges – trade union membership statistics', Trades Union Congress, [online], Available from: www.tuc.org.uk/blogs/good-news-bad-news-and-same-challenges-trade-union-membership-statistics [Accessed 28 June 2022].

Steffan B. (2021) 'Managing menopause at work: The contradictory nature of identity talk', *Gender, Work and Organization*, 28(1): 195–214.

Targett, R. and Beck, V. (2022) 'Menopause as a well-being strategy: Organizational effectiveness, gendered ageism and racism', *Post Reproductive Health*, 28(1): 23–7.

Trades Union Congress (2017) 'Gender in occupational safety and health', [online], Available from: www.tuc.org.uk/sites/default/files/GenderHS2 017.pdf [Accessed 28 June 2022].

Trades Union Congress (2022) 'Older workers after the pandemic: Creating an inclusive labour market', [online], Available from: www.tuc.org.uk/resea rch-analysis/reports/older-workers-after-pandemic-creating-inclusive-lab our-market [Accessed 28 June 2022].

University and College Union (2018) 'Supporting menopausal women at work', [online], Available from: www.ucu.org.uk/media/9973/Support ing-menopausal-women-at-work---briefing/pdf/Supporting_menopausa l_women_at_work.pdf [Accessed 28 June 2022].

UNISON (2021) 'Menopause: The menopause is a workplace issue: Guidance and model policy', [online], Available from: www.uni son.org.uk/content/uploads/2021/02/26305_menopause_guide-1.pdf [Accessed 28 June 2022].

Unite (2012) 'Negotiators' guide: Women's health, safety and well-being at work', [online], Available from: www.unitetheunion.org/media/1480/ womens-health-safety-well-being-at-work-unite-guide.pdf [Accessed 28 June 2022].

Valentini, C., Ihlen, Ø., Somerville, I., Raknes, K. and Davidson, S. (2020) 'Trade unions and lobbying: Fighting private interests while defending the public interest?', *International Journal of Communication*, 14: 4913–31.

Van der Heijden, B., Pak, K. and Santana, M. (2021) 'Menopause and sustainable career outcomes: A science mapping approach', *International Journal of Environmental Research and Public Health*, 18(23): 12559.

Wales TUC Cymru (2017) 'The menopause in the workplace: A toolkit for trade unionists', [online], Available from: www.tuc.org.uk/sites/defa ult/files/Menopause%20toolkit%20Eng%20FINAL.pdf [Accessed 28 June 2022].

Wallis, E., Stuart, M. and Greenwood, I. (2005) '"Learners of the workplace unite!" An empirical examination of the UK trade union learning representative initiative', *Work, Employment and Society*, 19(2): 283–304.

Yoeli, H., Macnaughton, J. and McLusky, S. (2021) 'Menopausal symptoms and work: A narrative review of women's experiences in casual, informal, or precarious jobs', *Maturitas*, 150: 14–21.

6

Spatial (In)justice and Hot Flushes in the Workplace: Some Musings and Provocations

Jo Brewis

Introduction

This chapter focuses on cis women's experiences of problematic hot flushes at work and how their shared workspaces are often beset with tensions around temperature and ventilation as a result. I draw loosely on Andreas Philippopoulos-Mihalopoulos' (2010, 2015, 2017, 2020) reading of spatial justice, and Sophie Watson's (2020) use of this concept to understand the Muslim practice of Wudu[1] in public spaces, to try to theorize shared organizational space as characterized by a series of injustices in this respect. These are generated, Philippopoulos-Mihalopoulos (2017, p 24) explains, as follows:

> '[T]here is something inalienable in our connection to space: we are all bodies vying for the same space, excluding other bodies along the way. We generate space, we are space, and we are constantly on the move, generating more space but also more conflict with other bodies.'

The data I use are taken from two projects. The first is an online survey that we ran in the summer of 2018 in conjunction with TUC Education on people's knowledge about menopause per se but also and more significantly its impact on their workplaces and them as individual workers. This attracted 5,399 respondents. The second project involved interviews and two surveys at Northshire, a pseudonymous NHS hospital trust in the UK. This was longitudinal, tracking the impact of the Trust's introduction of menopause guidance and an accompanying programme of support on its staff. The arguments I make are also informed by the anecdotes that Vanessa and I hear when sharing our ongoing research on menopause at work which centre on shared organizational space and the challenges of regulating temperature to suit everyone within this kind of space.

Hot flushes at work

During a July 2021 episode of the prime time BBC1 magazine programme *The One Show*, journalist and presenter Louise Minchin talked about her menopausal hot flushes, and a solution she had been able to implement at work. This she described as 'a few simple steps', as follows:

'It's been 20 years since I first presented BBC Breakfast and I have spent much of my time sitting on the famous red sofa. I love it but a few years ago it became a challenge when I began going through the menopause. At home, it triggered anxiety and terrible night sweats but it was also a problem at work. So imagine you're sitting on the BBC Breakfast sofa and there's six million people watching every day and you're feeling hot and bothered and you're really exposed. I talked to my boss about it and we keep the studio, when I'm in it, super cool. There's even a mark on the thermometer for Louise degrees.' (Quoted in Kelly, 2021)

Hot flushes are one of the most common menopausal symptoms. More than half of the women who self-identified as menopausal or post-menopausal (*n*=3914) in our TUC Education survey said they had experienced hot flushes, and 35 per cent said this was the most difficult symptom to manage at work (Beck, Brewis and Davies, 2020, pp 160–1). The National Institute for Health and Care Excellence (2015, p 73) also suggest that, for 75 per cent of women, this symptom endures into post-menopause and affects 25 per cent particularly badly. If we then consider that women in the global north are, as this volume makes very clear, working until or returning to work in greater numbers later in life, then it becomes easy to see that many women are having to navigate the difficulties that hot flushes present in the workplace.

As Louise Minchin's story suggests, hot flushes at work can be both embarrassing and physically uncomfortable. They can also have a knock-on effect for women's performance. For example, 18 per cent of the 8,578 US women questioned for the secondary data analysed by Whiteley et al (2013) said their hot flushes combined with other menopause symptoms to negatively affect their performance at work. Gartoulla et al (2016) surveyed 1,263 Australian women, finding that those reporting lower work ability were significantly more likely to report hot flushes and night sweats. Other research demonstrates that hot flushes can affect work ability and productivity, and make work tasks more stressful (Kronenberg, 1990; Park, Satoh and Kumashiro, 2008, 2011; Whiteley et al, 2013; Duijits et al, 2014; Griffiths and Hunter, 2015; Sarrel et al, 2015). In our own primary data, the first Northshire survey saw 68.3 per cent of those who reported having hot flushes saying they had a negative effect at work. In survey 2, the equivalent proportion was even higher, at 72 per cent.

Hot flushes can be exacerbated by inadequate ventilation, high temperatures, humidity and dryness at work (Putnam and Bochantin 2009; Jack et al, 2014; Kopenhager and Guidozzi, 2015). In fact 72 per cent of 300+ menopausal women who answered an Australian survey question about organizational support said they would appreciate having temperature control at work to enable them to cope with this symptom better (Hickey et al, 2017, p 206). These respondents, like those at Northshire, worked in hospitals. In our TUC Education survey, answers to a question about aspects of the workplace that made symptoms worse were dominated by high temperature (selected by 39.4 per cent), poor ventilation (35.2 per cent) and humidity (24.5 per cent). The Northshire surveys produced similar findings, with 79.7 per cent of those responding to the same question in survey 1 saying high temperatures at work made symptoms worse and 63.8 per cent saying the same for poor ventilation. In survey 2, 83.7 per cent identified high temperature, and 77.8 per cent poor ventilation, in the same regard. Certain kinds of workwear and uniform can be similarly problematic – including heavy, cumbersome or synthetic clothes as well as personal protective equipment like goggles or stab vests (Griffiths et al, 2006; Altmann, 2015).

There is by now a fairly well-established commentary on this and other environmental adjustments which can help to address the detrimental effects of hot flushes at work. The capacity to control temperature, as discussed in the Hickey et al study, is indexed here (Griffiths, Maclennan and Hassard, 2013; Fenton and Panay, 2014; Kopenhager and Guidozzi, 2015; Griffiths et al, 2016), as is having a fan or access to ventilation (Reynolds, 1999; Griffiths et al, 2006; Griffiths, MacLennan and Wong 2010; Griffiths, Maclennan and Hassard, 2013; Fenton and Panay, 2014; Griffiths and Hunter, 2015; Griffiths et al, 2016). The relevant commentary also identifies cold drinking water and adjustments to uniform or workwear so women can wear lighter and/or more breathable clothes to work. Jack et al (2016), finally, suggest that they should be able to relocate away from small or confined workspaces.

Women can take matters into their own hands if they don't receive adequate support of this kind, like those interviewed by Butler (2020, pp 702–3). Where her respondents worked in open plan spaces and/or air-conditioned environments with windows that wouldn't open, many worried that sweating due to a hot flush meant they would smell. As Butler suggests, they accommodated this by jamming internal doors open – even though this was against the rules, not to say the Health and Safety at Work Act 1974 – and sometimes breaking hinges so the doors wouldn't shut at all. One woman used an office move to her advantage for the same reason, consulting a friend who had access to the plans for the new space and then selecting a desk near the air vents to maximize airflow.

However, the recommendations around temperature control and ventilation to support working women who experience problematic hot flushes are likely to impact on their colleagues if they – like Louise Minchin and the women interviewed by Butler, and many, many others – share their workspace with others. Certainly Louise's positive experience of having her colleagues agree to keep the studio thermostat at 'Louise degrees' when she is on set is not one that all menopausal women share. This is where Philippopoulos-Mihalopoulos' and Watson's readings of spatial justice come in. Before I turn to those readings, though, I will briefly summarize the methodology used for the two empirical projects which I draw on here.

Methodology

The first of these projects was an online survey, also discussed in Chapter 5 by Vanessa, which we disseminated using personal and professional networks, academic mailing lists, TUC Education networks, social media and personal networks. This was funded via the

Economic and Social Research Council Impact Acceleration scheme at the University of Bristol. The survey was open between early June and late July 2018. Once we had excluded those who indicated that they didn't want their answers to be used in our analysis or didn't understand the survey's purpose, we arrived at a total sample size of 5,399. To the best of our knowledge this is the biggest academic survey to date on menopause at work which includes employees from a range of organizations. The survey was given full approval by the University of Bristol School of Management Research Ethics Committee. Findings from this survey are also reported in Beck, Brewis and Davies (2020, 2021).

The second was a year-long research project at Northshire NHS Foundation Trust, a pseudonym for the three hospitals where I conducted the surveys and the interviews. I was invited by the Chief Nurse at the Trust to run the project, as she was keen to find out how effective the menopause guidance and programme of support, which included workshops on HRT and mental health during menopause, was following implementation. We agreed the structure of the research with her team. As is mandatory with research involving NHS staff in the UK, the project received a positive opinion from the Health Research Authority (project number 25010) and, consequently, from The Open University Human Research Ethics Committee before data collection began. Vanessa, our collaborator and friend Andrea Davies and I designed a pre-launch event survey using Bristol Online Surveys to explore what staff at Northshire knew about menopause and to what extent and how it impacted them, their work and their workplace. It was entirely anonymous and attracted 84 respondents, from a total staff complement of 5,000.

After the guidance and the programme of support had been implemented, I then interviewed individual members of staff who had volunteered to take part at intervals of roughly three months. As is common with longitudinal research, there was some attrition during the process but I interviewed seven staff three times, one twice and two once. I ran a second online survey once the interviews had finished, 12 months after the launch of the guidance and support programme. This was intended as a comparator with the first baseline survey to get a wider picture of the impact of the intervention on staff at the Trust. Again it was entirely anonymous, and attracted 72 respondents. We used the basic reporting function in Jisc Online Surveys to analyse the quantitative data from the three surveys and a combination of NVivo and manual thematic coding to analyse the qualitative data.

In the following section, I present a discussion combining an overview of Philippopoulos-Mihalopoulos' and Watson's treatments of spatial justice with reference to our primary data to illustrate how the latter exemplify some of the key points of their arguments. As a preliminary, it was clear from the data that some participants who had hot flushes were well supported at work – for example, with the provision of desk fans or being able to move their seats in an office nearer to the door so the corridor provided some ventilation. However, many others experienced problems in this regard.

Discussion: spatial (in)justice and hot flushes at work

As indicated by the title of this chapter, my intention here is to offer some musings and provocations around how spatial justice might be relevant to understanding tensions at work around temperature and ventilation, using data from our research projects. I was initially intrigued by Philippopoulos-Mihalopoulos' concept after hearing my OU colleague Sophie Watson refer to it in a seminar in May 2019, because of his definition that spatial justice turns on '*the conflict between bodies that are moved by a desire to occupy the same space at the same time … the emergence of a negotiation between bodies*' (2015, p 3). I immediately thought it could be a helpful way of adding some theoretical heft to our grasp of this conflict as it plays out around hot flushes at work because it speaks precisely to the ways in which we navigate having to share space with each other.

Having now read a selection of Philippopoulos-Mihalopoulos' work more carefully, I realize that it is both extraordinarily rich and extremely complex, taking inspiration from Deleuze and Guattari, Luhmann, Spinoza and a range of other continental philosophers. He also works at the interstices between law and geography, and as such I am wrenching his ideas away from their intellectual home, perhaps illegitimately. As such I am not able to do anything like justice to Philippopoulos-Mihalopoulos' arguments, especially in the limited confines of a book chapter and my own intellectual deficiencies. My analysis then is only intended *as* provocative: it is a series of reflections on how we might start to talk about spatial conflicts over temperature and ventilation between menopausal women and their non-menopausal colleagues in a more theoretical way.

With these caveats in place, if we take off from the definition Philippopoulos-Mihalopoulos offers of spatial justice, the corollary is his observation that justice is 'spatial, corporeal, and generally material' (2015, p 3): it has to do with how we occupy space with our physical beings. He sites his theorizing in the law, but insists that it goes well beyond an exploration of legislation – instead law is acted out, performed, by bodies. This Philippopoulos-Mihalopoulos calls the 'lawscape'. In a workplace environment, we can I think conceive of this as how laws – but also organizational policy and prohibitions – are acted out. Examples include the resistance demonstrated by some of Butler's (2020) respondents to the legally mandated restrictions around fire doors at work as well as one of our TUC Education survey respondents who told us 'I got a plug in desk fan, but they're not really allowed'. Philippopoulos-Mihalopoulos suggests that the interaction between law and space in the lawscape can be more or less visibilized, or overt, giving the example of a no smoking sign in a public place as an example of visibilization. Here the space is obviously and explicitly regulated. But he adds that in the 'free, open space of an art gallery ... space retains a façade of ambling and *seemingly* unconstrained movement, free from legal presence' (2015, p 4 – emphasis added). This is invisibilization, because visitors to the gallery will likely accept that they need to be sensitive when they are viewing exhibitions and ensure they are not blocking others' lines of sight for extended periods of time: they cannot simply 'amble' along in 'unconstrained movement'.

Philippopoulos-Mihalopoulos gives another example of invisibilization of the law when he talks about a family home, and the comfort and cosiness it connotes. However, he adds that this, like the art gallery, is an example of how the lawscape 'dissimulates', as he puts it. In other words, a private home is also a legal space where forms of official regulation still apply. These include so-called home rights, which give a spouse the right to live in the family home even when it is their partner who legally owns the property. But these regulations are much less intensely present or overt than the example of the no smoking sign or his other instance of the prison. What we have here then is an interesting set of tensions between the law on the one hand and the materiality and elasticity of space on the other. The latter, for Philippopoulos-Mihalopoulos, suggests 'manoeuvring ... for the various bodies that constitute the lawscape to affect it in various ways'. These 'possibilities of resistance and negotiation' (2015, p 4) – which he also calls withdrawal – are much less apparent when law dissimulates, as it does in an art gallery or a home.

However, this is not to say that the law somehow becomes irrelevant in these spaces. And of course, in the workplace the law is much more likely to be explicit, to be visibilized – or striated, in one of Philippopoulos-Mihalopoulos' borrowings from Deleuze and Guattari. Our data bear this out. So, as a TUC Education survey respondent told us, she had tried to use a workplace policy to obtain a fan to ameliorate her hot flushes but the process 'required an O[ccupational] H[ealth and] S[afety sign off] to obtain. Ridiculous and costly process'. Another complained about 'no[t] being allowed a desk fan without an OHS!'. A third commented that

> '[A]ll of the fans were taken away from our office to reduce costs and you have to have a medical reason to get one back[:] this shouldn't be the case, women shouldn't have to shout about being menopausal. After all it is often a private issue to get access to fans to help cool them down.'

In these examples, then, visibilized workplace policy and the associated bureaucracy are invoked to deter requests for physical alterations to shared space.

Other data we have gathered suggest the law might actually be acted out in such a way as to produce *over*-visibilization in workplaces when it comes to temperature regulation. In other words, our participants suggested that others' behaviours amplified existing policies well beyond the letter of the law. An example is this comment from a nurse at Northshire:

> 'I have a small USB fan that does help alleviate hot flushes although Matron did insist it was PAT tested. I have spoken to [the] PAT testing team and it is not appropriate. Matron has actually attended seminars as a manager to help staff with menopause symptoms … I give up!'

Here then we see how a clinical line manager at Northshire acts out organizational policy – that is, constructs and reconstructs the lawscape – to make what should arguably be a simple process of requesting a USB fan into something which was needlessly complicated. This was despite the fact that this manager had been to sessions on supporting their team through menopause.

Further to such actings out in the lawscape, Philippopoulos-Mihalopoulos posits that our desire for spatial justice is what he refers to as a '*conative* characteristic of the body' – its will to survive and thrive, to continue, quite literally, to be (2015, pp 7–8). He suggests that this, combined with 'the irreducibility of corporeal emplacement in space', means any claim to be here 'rises above the [letter of the] law while relying on it: the law defines who is at any point to be here and only to a very basic extent who can claim to be here' (2010, p 202). This is because only a single body can occupy a single space at any given moment, and therefore my claim to be here – and to take up space in the way that I see fit – is always and inexorably a claim which conflicts with yours. Legal regulations of any kind will only provide the simplest of guidance as to who has rights to occupy any specific space at any given time, and to occupy it as they wish to. The rest is negotiated via the lawscape.

Spatial justice, then,

> is an exigent ethical exercise that demands a radical gesture of *withdrawal*: to withdraw before the claim of the other is what [it] demands ... [It involves] allowing the position of the other to make her territory out of my position, it is '*the movement of taking leave*': 'I withdraw from the space on which I am and from my desire to your space'. (2010, pp 202, 210, 213)

What this means then, as we can see already in the extracts from our data, is that the human bodies inhabiting space are also engaged in ongoing and sometimes very tricky negotiations over the terms of its occupation. To withdraw effectively means to give someone else the freedom to occupy a space however they choose to, and includes (but is not limited to) physically leaving that space.

Philippopoulos-Mihalopoulos writes that 'we populate space with conflict and its violence and we position ourselves in relation to it', describing this violence as 'casual, quotidian ... deeply entrenched and invisibilised' (2017, pp 21–2). As groups of human beings, we are, he argues, always 'one body and another body. And then, right in the middle of this, the desire of movement: I want to be where you are, exactly *there*, exactly *then*' (2010, p 210). An ongoing conflict between one of my Northshire interview respondents and her colleague seems to me to exemplify the conflict Philippopoulos-Mihalopoulos talks about here over shared space:

'I get very hot, I work in an office that is very hot. I have a fan on from the minute I get in until the minute I go home. I sit next to somebody who won't have the window open which I find immensely infuriating because I can't take clothes off: they can add clothes, but I cannot. So we work in a temporary building which was a temporary building I think about eight years ago, ten years ago, and so all the heating elements, all the hot water pipes for that building run through our office. And there's probably one, two, there's about four of us that are of our age that are going through the change, but I have to have the fan on because it's just too hot.'

'So, yeah, I have a real, I get very frustrated with the temperature of the office and there's a lot of us in the office, so there's probably 16 of us in the office working on desks, so 16 sets of computers, 16 sets of lights.'

'[A]nd people say turn the lights off, but I can't see without the lights because I sit in a corner, so I cannot see my computer if the lights are not on, so the heat that's generated from lights.'

'Especially when you sit next to somebody who won't open a window. Even in the summer she doesn't like it open.'

'We open the window when she goes out.'

As this series of extracts suggests, the single occupant of the shared office who refuses to have the window open (but equally will not move to a desk further away from this source of ventilation, as we will see later) positions herself in a violent way in relation to her colleagues. It appears to be her preferences which dictate how space is occupied for all 16 staff who work in this area, which also appear to be 'casual, quotidian' and 'deeply entrenched', as Philippopoulos–Mihalopoulos suggests.

Similar data from the TUC Education survey include the following, in open text comments about aspects of work that made menopause symptoms more trying:

'The office is hot and stuffy and not all the windows open. Other workers complain they are cold but they can put on clothes, I cannot sit in my bra and pants.'

'Having to work with unsympathetic male managers and colleagues who think that simple requests to adjust the temperature in the office [are] a burden – plus being told to "take clothes off" when experiencing a hot flush is just not acceptable!'

'The temperature in my office is 26 degrees. There are 11 desks[,] 11 [PCs and a] photocopier. Main server. Fridge freezer[,] low ceiling. Horrendous lighting. Two windows. Three double radiators. And the selfish staff that I share this hell hole with. 26 degrees and two members of staff want the windows closed ... sitting at their desks with their fleeces on. Oh and electric fan heaters under the desks. The office manager is male[,] the rest female ... he doesn't like to get involved with all this women stuff ... I am at my lowest ebb right now.'

In this last extract especially, as in the comments from the Northshire interviewee, we can see the negative effects of spatial injustice – where two colleagues prevail over the remaining nine and the line manager refuses to intercede – very clearly.

Philippopoulos-Mihalopoulos also emphasizes that any negotiations around space are corporeal as well as verbal. Here I imagine the ways that people physically take up or inhabit space – manspreading springs to mind as an example, as does loud chatter or music in a shared office or a train carriage. He adds that the bodies involved aren't just human, but non-human as well: for my purposes this would include doors, windows, fans and thermostats as well as law, organizational regulations, uniforms and other prescribed workwear. And our data seem to point to corporeal negotiations of this kind, where individuals do not verbally express their temperature and ventilation preferences to colleagues but instead take action to suit them. As respondents to the TUC Education survey commented,

'[I t]ry to keep windows open, but very often colleagues would close them!'

'[I] have been made to feel [like a] demanding nuisance asking for a desk fan. Had to wait weeks for one (in winter) and [was] made to feel a proper pest! I borrowed one and my manager (a female) took it an[d] put it on a high shelf out of my reach.'

'[I work in an] open plan office with erratic heating so people turn the thing on and off.'

One respondent suggested that one of her colleagues had gone even further and actually invaded her physical space in these corporeal negotiations. She said that he '[a]ctively comments on my flushes to other colleagues and clients. Blew in my face to see if it cooled me down'.

Moreover, and again as foreshadowed in some of the foregoing data extracts, spatial justice is not an interaction between or negotiation of equals. As Philippopoulos-Mihalopoulos writes, 'The stronger, more powerful bodies pull this continuum down, a body weight crunching the plane, making it fold and unfold in undulating configurations determined by the bodies themselves ... [the continuum is] tilted, unequal, biased' (2017, p 28). This is illustrated beautifully by Watson's (2020) discussion of Wudu, which is the ritual washing of head, neck, hands, arms and feet before prayer in Islam. This is a highly structured practice and can only take place in certain spaces. As Watson points out,

'The performance of Wudu in modern city life can be challenging for Muslims, particularly in work places where there is no easy access to water, or where for women, there is a necessity to share intimate spaces and facilities. Arguably, Wudu reconfigures private/public boundaries and challenges normative notions as to appropriate conduct in public, since in most Western cultures intimate embodied practices are confined to private space, whereas Wudu brings parts of the body [the feet especially] into public places.' (pp 171–2)

There are also logistical challenges for practising Muslims in public spaces in the global north – shared bathrooms may not be clean, they do not usually have bidets and there may be insufficient space to perform the ritual. Then there is the question of timing; whether someone's lunch break at work, for example, allows sufficient time to include Wudu, prayer *and* eating a meal. In addition, Muslims often face a lack of understanding and at times hostility from non-Muslims with whom they share bathroom space, perhaps because they spill water when washing their feet or because they are required to gargle with water and rinse inside the nose as part of Wudu, which others might find unpleasant. Indeed Watson interviewed Muslims who 'reported feeling conscious of the disapproval of non-Muslim others, particularly when Wudu is practised in the sink, and they see water on the floor or someone cleaning/drying the floor' (2020, p 175). Equally, where gender-specific washing facilities and prayer rooms are provided at work, non-Muslims may perceive this as an unacceptable form of special treatment.

Like women experiencing hot flushes who find informal, sometimes non-sanctioned solutions to the problem of high temperature and inadequate ventilation at work, some Muslims use strategies to allow them to practise Wudu in difficult environments. So taxi drivers might carry water containers in their car boots so they can wash while sitting on the car's bumper, for example. Others avoid the ritual altogether in public, such as by using Khuffain, special leather socks which can be put on at home in the mornings after Wudu and which ensure that one's feet are symbolically clean for prayer during the working day.

What is especially significant here is not just the very clear tensions around specific ways of occupying public space, not just the '*conflict between bodies that are moved by a desire to occupy the same space at the same time*' that Philippopoulos-Mihalopoulos (2015, p 3) identifies. It is also and precisely the inequality of this conflict, the 'tilted' plane on which it plays out. Watson comments as follows:

'typically, for Muslims practising Wudu [in public spaces in the Global North], there is the necessity to assert their practice in the face of rules and regulations and accepted modes of conduct that have been set by others – implicitly or explicitly. As such it is an articulation in the context of unequal power relations.' (2020, p 184)

We have already seen this 'tiltedness' playing out in our menopause at work data in respondents' efforts to request environmental adjustments at work and finding managers unsupportive. But we can also see it in comments from the Northshire respondent quoted earlier whose colleague refuses to have a window open at work even in very hot weather:

'I think the office, they've moved me, so I don't have the same problems. So since I've moved, and we've had the hot weather, that person hasn't had their window open. And it's been 26 [degrees] outside. And I just think "do you know what?", and they're sat there with a cardigan on, but the rest of the office is absolutely sweltering.'

'And there's always an excuse "oh my back, oh my back's stiff, I can't come in", you know, it's very predictable. So, but we should move that person, but that person can't be moved because they've always sat there. So hang on a minute, you know, you're going to let another ten people suffer.'

What I see here, and in other data extracts where it is colleagues as opposed to managers who prove combative both verbally and corporeally around temperature and ventilation at work, is a kind of sedimentation of custom and practice ('they've always sat there') into Philippopoulos-Mihalopoulos' tiltedness. This is in contradistinction to formal inequality in the shape of authority structures at work or indeed wider cultural inequality in the case of non-Muslim intolerance of Muslims practising Wudu in public bathrooms. There is also evidence of line managers' reluctance to intervene to open up any discussion of spatial justice in this regard. The commentary from the TUC Education respondent who said she was at her 'lowest ebb right now' because of the temperature in her office is another example of such recalcitrance.

Watson adds that any refusal of Wudu in public places denies Muslims the capacity to engage in a ritual which is at the very centre of their religious observance, and thus effectively bans them from the same places. Equally, it is not unimaginable that menopausal women suffering hot flushes may seek to leave their jobs because of spatial injustice related to workplace temperature and ventilation. Certainly Evandrou et al (2021) have already suggested, based on analysis of two successive waves of the National Child Development Study, that women with at least one problematic menopausal symptom at the age of 50 are 43 per cent more likely to have quit work altogether by the time they reach 55. Bryson et al (2022) reach similar conclusions about women who experience early menopause – that is, before the age of 45. Their analysis of data from the same survey suggests that, when these women enter their 50s, their employment rate is some 9 percentage points lower than that of their counterparts.

Next I wrap this chapter up with a short conclusion.

Conclusion

It is not my intention to offer concrete solutions to the problems identified in this chapter but rather, as indicated earlier, to shed some tentative theoretical light on the pervasive problem of shared physical space when temperature and ventilation are at issue. In suggesting that Philippopoulos-Mihalopoulos' and Watson's discussions of spatial justice serve this purpose, I have also modestly gone beyond their analyses in arguing that, first, lawscapes can perhaps be mobilized in workplaces, especially by those with formal authority, in such a way as to *over*-striate them; and, second, custom and practice can sediment into a form of tiltedness such that inequality emerges simply because of the ways that things have been done over a period of time.

We have also seen evidence that others can and do accommodate the needs of women suffering from menopausal hot flushes at work in Louise Minchin's story and in some of our primary data. But this chapter has concentrated on the opposite – spatial *in*justice where one side appears unwilling to question their position on temperature and ventilation in shared workspaces, much less to contemplate even a moderate form of withdrawal, in Philippopoulos-Mihalopoulos' terms.

As such, Philippopoulos-Mihalopoulos has two relevant observations to make. First, he argues that, in situations where shared space is creating tensions,

'One needs to go back to the lawscape and question one's position. Acceptance is enough as a start, and might lead somewhere, but needs concerted efforts on all sides to go further and deeper. The lawscape needs to be re-oriented. Conflict will not disappear – and luckily, nor will difference. But the discourse might change, and the emerging register might become more sharp, less accommodating.' (2020, p 7)

His remarks here are interesting in terms of returning to the lawscape. Even though lawscapes in workplaces do tend to be more visibilized, there is in fact no legislation – in the UK at least – for minimum or maximum temperatures in organizations. The Health and Safety at Work Act 1974 simply ordains that temperatures should be comfortable for staff and fresh, clean air must be provided. These kinds of stipulations are of course very open to interpretation, so any references to the law in this regard are unlikely to be helpful for negotiations over heat and ventilation at work. Some organizations will have their own policies of course – at The Open University, for example, the Estates department is expected to maintain office temperatures at between 20°C and 23°C. Still, this is phrased as being 'desirable' as opposed to mandatory. Moreover, and as this chapter has demonstrated, the lawscape is how we perform the law – or the policy – as opposed to the law or policy itself. As such, returning to the lawscape necessitates precisely the reorientation that Philippopoulos-Mihalopoulos indexes: collectively we need to make 'concerted efforts' to 'go further and deeper' to understand the different positions we may inhabit in this scape.

Indeed Philippopoulos-Mihalopoulos also writes that 'Spatial justice ... [is] a moderator of the desire to expand like a gas and take up all available space. Spatial justice questions the limits of our desires' (2020, p 6). This serves, I think, as a useful aide-mémoire to all of us around the physical limits of our shared world, in workplaces as elsewhere, and therefore suggests the broader implications of this concept for menopause as an organizational issue and employment relations more generally. Riach and Jack (2021) suggest that, for women who are able to, working from home is often a good solution to the difficulties symptoms like hot flushes can create. And of course the COVID-19 pandemic has taught us a great deal about how to make arrangements like this function as effectively as possible for all concerned. But this is not possible for all menopausal employees, and we also know that women are over-represented in sectors like health and social care which often require physical presence at work.

And, because organizational space must of necessity be shared with others, whether we work in open plan areas or not, open discussions which acknowledge this issue and provide information about how it can affect members of certain groups (including but not limited to menopausal women – staff with multiple sclerosis, diabetes, fibromyalgia or thyroid conditions, inter alia, can also be very sensitive to heat) may serve to move co-located workers closer to some form of acceptable compromise. It will also make these groups feel listened to and seen.

Note
[1] Sometimes rendered as Wudhu.

References

Altmann, R. (2015) *A New Vision for Older Workers*, [online], London, Department for Work and Pensions, 11 March, Available from: https://www.gov.uk/government/publications/a-new-vision-for-older-workers-retain-retrain-recruit [Accessed 4 April 2022].

Beck, V., Brewis, J. and Davies, A. (2020) 'The remains of the taboo: Experiences, attitudes, and knowledge about menopause in the workplace', *Climacteric*, 23(2): 158–64.

Beck, V., Brewis, J. and Davies, A. (2021) 'Women's experiences of menopause at work and performance management', *Organization*, 28(3): 510–20.

Bryson, A., Conti, G., Hardy, G., Hardy, R., Peycheva, D. and Sullivan, A. (2022) 'The consequences of early menopause and menopause symptoms for labour market participation', *Social Science & Medicine*, 293: 114676.

Butler, C. (2020) 'Managing the menopause through "abjection work": When boobs can become embarrassingly useful, again', *Work, Employment and Society*, 34(4): 696–712.

Duijits, S.F.A., van Egmond, M.P., Spelten, E., van Muijen, P., Anema, J.R. and van der Beek, A.J. (2014) 'Physical and psychosocial problems in cancer survivors beyond return to work: A systematic review', *Psycho-Oncology*, 23(5): 481–92.

Evandrou, M., Falkingham, J., Qin, M. and Vlachantoni, A. (2021) 'Menopausal transition and change in employment: Evidence from the National Child Development Study', *Maturitas,* 143: 96–104.

Fenton, A. and Panay, N. (2014) 'Editorial. Menopause and the workplace', *Climacteric*, 17(4): 317–18.

Gartoulla, P., Bell, R.J., Worsley, R. and Davis, S.R. (2016) 'Menopausal vasomotor symptoms are associated with poor self-assessed work ability', *Maturitas*, 87: 33–9.

Griffiths, A., Ceausu, I., Depyperec, H., Lambrinoudaki, I., Mueck, A., Pérez-López, F.R. et al (2016) 'EMAS recommendations for conditions in the workplace for menopausal women', *Maturitas*, 85: 79–81.

Griffiths, A., Cox, S., Griffiths, R. and Wong, V. (2006) *Women Police Officers: Ageing, Work & Health,* [online] Report for the British Association for Women in Policing, Institute of Work, Health and Organisations, University of Nottingham, Available from: https://docplayer.net/49897457-Women-police-officers-ageing-work-health.html [Accessed 4 April 2022].

Griffiths, A. and Hunter, M.S. (2015) 'Psychosocial factors and the menopause: The impact of the menopause on personal and working life', in S.C. Davies (ed) *Annual Report of the Chief Medical Officer. The Health of the 51%: Women, 2014,* [online], London: Department of Health, pp 109–20, Available from: https://assets.publishing.service.gov.uk/governm ent/uploads/system/uploads/attachment_data/file/595439/CMO_ann ual_report_2014.pdf [Accessed 4 April 2022].

Griffiths, A., MacLennan, S. and Wong, Y.Y.V. (2010) *Women's Experience of Working through the Menopause*, Report for the British Occupational Health Research Foundation, Institute of Work, Health and Organisations, University of Nottingham, UK [Accessed 26 July 2023].

Griffiths, A., Maclennan, S. and Hassard, J. (2013) 'Menopause and work: An electronic survey of employees' attitudes in the UK', *Maturitas*, 76(2): 155–9.

Hickey, M., Riach, K., Kachoiue, R. and Jack, G. (2017) 'No sweat: Managing menopausal symptoms at work', *Journal of Psychosomatic Obstetrics and Gynaecology*, 38(3): 202–9.

Jack, G., Pitts, M., Riach, K., Bariola, E., Schapper, J. and Sarrel, P. (2014) *Women, Work and the Menopause: Releasing the Potential of Older Professional Women,* [online], final project report, La Trobe University, Melbourne, Australia, Available from: https://womenworkandthemenopause.com/final-project-pdf-download/ [Accessed 4 April 2022].

Jack, G., Riach, K., Bariola, E., Pitts, M., Schapper, J. and Sarrel, P. (2016) 'Menopause in the workplace: What employers should be doing', *Maturitas,* 85: 88–95.

Kelly, H. (2021) 'Louise Minchin opens up on "problem" at work on BBC Breakfast "It triggered anxiety"', *Daily Express*, [online] 1 July, Available from: https://www.express.co.uk/showbiz/tv-radio/1457225/Louise-Minchin-problem-BBC-Breakfast-anxiety-menopause-video [Accessed 4 April 2022].

Kopenhager, T. and Guidozzi, F. (2015) 'Working women and the menopause', *Climacteric*, 18(3): 372–5.

Kronenberg, F. (1990) 'Hot flashes: Epidemiology and physiology', *Annals of the New York Academy of Sciences*, 592: 52–86.

National Institute for Health and Care Excellence (2015) *Menopause: Full Guideline*, [online] 12 November, Available from: https://www.nice.org.uk/guidance/ng23 [Accessed 4 April 2022].

Park, M.K., Satoh, N. and Kumashiro, M. (2008) 'Mental workload under time pressure can trigger frequent hot flashes in menopausal women', *Industrial Health*, 46(3): 261–8.

Park, M.K., Satoh, N. and Kumashiro, M. (2011) 'Effects of menopausal hot flashes on mental workload', *Industrial Health*, 49(5): 566–74.

Philippopoulos-Mihalopoulos, A. (2010) 'Spatial justice: Law and the geography of withdrawal', *International Journal of Law in Context*, 6(3): 201–16.

Philippopoulos-Mihalopoulos, A. (2015) *Spatial Justice: Body, Lawscape, Atmosphere*, Oxford: Routledge.

Philippopoulos-Mihalopoulos, A. (2017) 'Spatial justice in a world of violence', in Butler, C. and Mussawir, E. (eds) *Spaces of Justice: Peripheries, Passages, Appropriations*, Oxford: Routledge, pp 21–36.

Philippopoulos-Mihalopoulos, A. (2020) 'The inconclusive spatial justice', in Watson, S. (ed) *Spatial Justice in the City*, Oxford, Routledge, pp 1–7. Author accepted manuscript, [online], Available from: https://westminsterresearch. westminster.ac.uk/item/qvxw5/the-inconclusive-spatial-justice [Accessed 4 April 2022].

Putnam, L. and Bochantin, J. (2009) 'Gendered bodies: negotiating normalcy and support', *Negotiation and Conflict Management Research*, 2(1): 57–73.

Reynolds, F. (1999) 'Distress and coping with hot flushes at work: Implications for counsellors in occupational settings', *Counselling Psychology Quarterly*, 12(4): 353–61.

Riach, K. and Jack, G. (2021) 'Women's health in/and work: Menopause as an intersectional experience', *International Journal of Environmental Research and Public Health*, 18(20). doi: 10.3390/ijerph182010793.

Sarrel, P., Portman, D., Lefebvre, P., Lafeuille, M.H., Grittner, A.M., Fortier, J., Gravel, J., Duh, M.S. and Aupperle, P.M. (2015) 'Incremental direct and indirect costs of untreated vasomotor symptoms', *Menopause*, 22(3): 260–6.

Watson, S. (2020) 'Differentiating water: Cultural practices and contestations', in Watson, S. (ed) *Spatial Justice in the City*, Oxford: Routledge, pp 167–96.

Whiteley, J., DiBonaventura, M.D., Wagner, J.-S., Alvir, J. and Shah, S. (2013) 'The impact of menopausal symptoms on quality of life, productivity, and economic outcomes', *Journal of Women's Health*, 22(11): 983–90.

7

Menopause and the Possibilities of Male Allyship

Hannah Bardett, Kathleen Riach and Gavin Jack

Introduction

In this chapter, we reflect on the possibilities of male allyship for educating about, advocating for and supporting menopausal transition at work as a form of gender or menopausal equality. An ally 'is any person that actively promotes and aspires to advance the culture of inclusion through intentional, positive and conscious efforts that benefit people as a whole' (Atcheson, 2018, np).

A variety of practices seek to reduce discrimination and inequality surrounding menopausal transition at work including supervisor or management training, use of occupational health and safety risk assessments to provide suitable accommodations, or the inclusion of menopause in HR and employee health and well-being policies, programmes and activities inter alia (Jack et al, 2016; Hardy, Griffiths and Hunter, 2019; Atkinson et al, 2021a). Much of the scholarly work regarding the nature and benefits of such practices has been based on data generated from individual women and their reported experience of menopause inside and outside the workplace (for example Beck, Brewis and Davies, 2020; Atkinson et al, 2021b), or managers of different genders regarding their attitudes or experience of training to support menopause at work (for example Hardy, Griffiths and Hunter, 2019). A central insight that traverses this work to date is that menopause is a site of gendered ageism (see, for example, Riach, Loretto and Krekula, 2015). This mode of inequality is socially constituted, situated and marked in multiple ways by relations between people and crucially also by the gendered and gendering dynamics of organizational life (Jack, Riach and Bariola, 2019). Reflecting on this insight, our chapter presents the findings of a small study that seeks to understand how men may engage with menopause at work with two particular foci in mind. First, to shed light on menopause equality work as a relational phenomenon based on the perspectives of a sample of male respondents. And second, to consider the prospective possibilities and challenges for men to act as workplace allies for working women going through menopause and to promote inclusive workplace environments.

We begin from a relational premise that men's perceptions of menopause invariably shape women's experience. Yet relatively few studies to date have addressed this topic, and those that do are typically focused on couples within familial settings. Zhang et al (2020) suggest that male spouses' views can affect both women's symptoms of menopause and their attitudes towards it, while the US-based Men's Attitudes Toward Menopause (MATE) study (Parish et al, 2019) reported that 75 per cent of men felt they were influential on decisions their partner made surrounding treatment for or lifestyle changes due to menopausal symptoms. Other studies highlight men's limited knowledge and understanding of menopause (Hidiroglu et al, 2014), despite a desire to support those experiencing it (Caçapava Rodolpho et al, 2016). While illustrating the importance of exploring perceptions of menopause beyond menopausal women, these studies focus on intimate and private relationships, rather than those that play out in public/institutional spaces such as the workplace. This is significant given that men in workplace settings may be unlikely to proactively seek information about menopause and may display a lack of understanding (though this is not the sole preserve of men), while women may be less likely to share their menopausal experiences or disclose, often due to fear of stigmatization, ridicule or questions over their performance (Jack, Riach and Bariola, 2019; Beck, Brewis and Davies, 2020).

We specifically explore the possibilities for young men to support menopausal transition at work through their engagement with the concept of allyship. However, in doing so, we seek to also critically reflect on the concept of allyship through engaging with an under-investigated male and workplace-related perspective on menopause. As noted at the outset of the chapter, allyship refers to a personal ethos and set of actions that promote an inclusive workplace culture.

Within the media and professional press, there has been increasing use of the term 'ally' surrounding workplace settings generally (for example Corbett, 2020; Melaku et al, 2020) and menopause specifically (such as Bloomberg, 2022; Where Women Work, 2022). This trend warrants further attention in terms of what the dynamics of allyship – and particularly young male allyship – may bring to ensuring menopausal transition is both recognized and supported in organizations. This chapter draws together literature on the menopause at work, recent debates about allyship from management studies, and a small empirical study of six young men on the precipice of joining the full-time labour market to investigate the possibilities and ambivalences of male allyship for educating about, advocating for and supporting menopausal transition at work.

Who does the 'work' of menopause at work? From women's self-advocacy to male champions to allies

Historically, menopause mirrors other research agendas surrounding ageing that have traditionally been dominated by a biomedical paradigm and approach to studying and understanding menopause. This has had the effect of restricting scholarly attention to a few disciplinary fields and prioritizing a medicalized, individualized and acontextual discourse surrounding menopause (Jack, Riach and Bariola, 2019). In recent years, however, this has changed. The last decade in particular has seen a significant rise in interest – both public and scholarly – in women's experience of menopause at work, with more attention on this topic coming from business and management academics (for example Jack, Riach and Bariola, 2019; Butler, 2020; Atkinson et al, 2021a,b; Steffan and Potočnik, 2022). A particular feature of this increased attention is that scholars are seeking to place women's experience of menopause into context, and to view it as a social and relational, as much as an individually experienced, embodied phenomenon. And while scholars have noted that menopausal experience is a gendered phenomenon – that is to say, subject to dominant social norms and understandings of the cis female body in organizational contexts – it is also embodied and interpreted in variegated ways at the intersections of multiple social markers, such as gender, race and class, and within and across different masculinities, femininities and sexualities (Riach and Jack, 2021). Following from these insights, we can consider the possibilities and potential ambivalences of male allyship in relation to menopause as a site of gendered relationalities in which multiple masculinities may also shape differing expectations and experiences of being a male ally, which in turn rebounds into the menopausal sphere.

This insight is illustrated with great clarity in Tienari and Taylor's (2019) essay in which they reflect upon their shared and different relationships to feminism as (white male) academics and allies, in relation to their work practices and identities. Noting that men's engagement with feminism 'will always be a contested issue' (2019, p 956), they articulate the different positions that men may and do take with respect to feminism, identifying their own on a kind of continuum from actively supportive (Taylor) to more deliberately directly engaged and declarative (Tienari). The different positions manifest around their own differences from mainstream management scholars, from female feminists and from each other as men engaging with feminism. Such relational differences underscore the fact that male allyship is no one thing, and in the particular case of men and feminism in academia, that 'adopting the label of feminist remains an area of disagreement, an open question, related to how we see ourselves as academics and as men' (Tienari and Taylor, 2019, p 957). What then might these concerns look like in relation to recognizing and supporting menopause at work?

In our experience of discussing menopause in the workplace, a repeated pattern has been that the call to support menopause at work has come from the ground up. In other words, it is usually cis women experiencing menopausal symptoms that come together to advocate for themselves within their workplaces as a previously unheard group in these organizations. This could take the form of informal group meetings at, for example, a menopause café, a movement started in 2017 in the UK by Rachel Weiss that has now spread across the world (see Gather to eat cake, drink and discuss menopause (menopausecafe. net)). It could also involve a more formal discussion or collaboration with HR or their line managers to gather information and knowledge and cultivate good practice in supporting staff going through menopausal transition.

While often a positive way to introduce the topic of menopause at work into organizational cultures, such approaches have their limitations. This is not a criticism of the women seeking to effect change in their organizations, nor of organizations who are open to respond to and support proactive employees. The critical issue here is that such approaches are reliant on specific people, rather than specific roles, to make a change. On the one hand, the sustainability and embedding of menopause at work in policy, practice and behaviour may be limited through the reliance on specific people. But more significantly, these approaches often carry the cost of placing additional labour onto a specific group: women going through menopause. The additional labour may take the form of tasks or work that go above and beyond these employees' formal roles. This work may also be on top of the informal emotional labour of negotiating gendered-ageist stereotypes that women may encounter alongside menopausal transition (Jack, Riach and Bariola, 2019).

Similar concerns have already been raised in previous studies looking at who does the 'work' of gender equality, and of diversity management, within organizations (Lorbiecki and Jack, 2000). Commentaries surrounding gender equality, for example, have repeatedly highlighted how it is those facing discrimination and inequality who are then expected to transform and enact change not only for themselves, but for others in the workplace. Mavin (2008, p s82) has also noted this when recognizing how the language of female solidarity often belies distinctly gendered sub-tones and disproportionate expectations. Here, placing responsibility for gender inequality on women is fraught, especially when organizational cultures can create divisions and conflict among women. For instance, organizational cultures may 'polarize' individual senior women as either 'good' (the woman who is actively involved in supporting other women), or as 'bad' (the woman who has achieved a senior management position by 'selling out' other women).

In an attempt to shift this responsibility, a top-down approach has emerged, whereby those in prominent leadership positions both recognize and take responsibility for gender inequality in their organizations. For example, the 'champion model' presents a counterpoint to the diffusion of responsibility and accountability for equality through calling on leaders or those in high profile positions to commit to equality or a particular diversity concern. A number of initiatives such as the Male Champions of Change model, introduced in Australia in 2010 (now the Champions of Change Coalition that also includes women), commit these stakeholders to work towards improving women's leadership opportunities and experiences through individual and collective influence. Such an approach has proven highly palatable across a variety of industries, particularly those dominated by men in senior positions, such as law (for example The Law Society, 2018).

Yet there are identified paradoxes and ambivalences associated with such models. This is despite the fact that more recent 'champions' initiatives have sought to be more gender inclusive, and that the language of internal organizational champions has proven popular in relation to menopause at work, where it has referred to people across the organizational hierarchy. For one, the Male Champions model may be seen as providing a way for men to align themselves (problematically) with the language of feminism while maintaining normative expectations of heroic leadership (Kelan and Wratil, 2018). Rather than transform behaviours, the championing model may reproduce gendered hierarchies and relations at work alongside the masculinist trope of the heroic individual leader (Kelan, 2018). Without care, the champion may easily fall into becoming a 'male saviour' figure (Kelan and Wratil, 2018), echoed in studies that highlight the expected reciprocity from such activities. As de Vries (2015, p 29) comments in her study of female and male executives leading gender change, 'Champion building was a two-way process that could be embraced or resisted – at least by the men. And for men who chose to embrace the role there was a dividend – the gratitude of women'. There have also been suggestions that focussing on leaders as champions may be less influential than focussing on middle managers who are often more important enablers or gatekeepers of gender (in)equality (Lansu, Bleijenbergh and Benschop, 2020).

To counter the aforementioned critiques, a recent third position of allyship seeks to balance support with rendering visible the labour and privilege involved in the work of equality. Originating from social justice and activism predominantly surrounding race, the adoption of the discourse of allyship has begun to emerge as an increasingly popular way to discuss workforce equality. Madsen, Townsend and Scribner's (2020, p 242) survey that included 80 responses from men refers to: 'allyship as being part of the dominant group, which provides allies with the ability to draw on social capital not available to marginalised individuals that can then be leveraged to create equity for marginalised groups'.

A recent *Harvard Business Review* article (Johnson and Smith, 2018, np) similarly suggested that allies were 'members of an advantaged group committed to building relationships with women, expressing as little sexism in their own behavior as possible, understanding the social privilege conferred by their gender, and demonstrating active efforts to address gender inequities at work and in society'.

Approaches to this can vary, from broad culture change programmes to more individual behaviour change approaches with men (Sawyer and Valerio, 2018). At the same time, many accounts stress that allyship work should focus on positive actions that support women or minorities generally, rather than on practices that explicitly confront oppression or privilege (Sumerau et al, 2021). For example, this might include bystander intervention training or using 'hard' data to encourage onboarding (see, for example, Anicha, Burnett and Bilen-Green, 2015). Madsen, Townsend and Scribner (2020) also note challenges to allyship where men who identify as allies might feel their own gender is held against them, while other accounts point to the potential backlash men may face when undertaking allyship (Anicha, Burnett and Bilen-Green, 2015). These findings echo some of the experiences of Taylor and Tienari (2019) as noted earlier and highlight the need to onboard powerful stakeholders, while not underplaying the experience of structural marginalization many groups with significantly less power face.

Popular coverage of menopause at work also draws in places on the language of allyship. The extent to which the turn to allyship in menopause equality work is aligned with the social justice roots of the discourse is less obvious. The consequence of this is that the extent to which allyship marks a distinct approach to menopause at work, and the challenges that manifest when allyship becomes part of a broader discussion surrounding menopause at work, are unclear. To begin exploring this empirically, we suggest that two elements can be seen as central to understanding the potential for male allyship when supporting menopausal transition at work. First is the need to be sensitive to the 'starting position' of potential allies in terms of their knowledge, mis/perceptions and experience of equality (Casey, 2010). Second is recognizing that the 'confrontation work' associated with allyship is not just situated in gender or being a man (Drury and Kaiser, 2014), but also across a variety of situated identity dynamics that can include age, position in the labour market or experience of the working environment. To explore this further, we turn to our empirical study to ask: how do young men expect to become male allies for menopausal equality at work?

Research design: young men talk menopause

We invited six men in their early twenties who had either recently completed or nearly completed their university degrees, and their mothers to take part in a two-step interview study. Coming from a prestigious institution, the socialized expectation was that participants would enter white collar professional settings. The research design first involved a short, 30–45-minute semi-structured interview between the first author, Hannah, and the male respondent, followed by an invitation for them to have a conversation with their mother or primary female caregiver (all respondents chose their mothers) around questions that sought to elicit a discussion of menopause and work. It was decided not to request a recording of these discussions but instead to focus on whether and how respondents narrated the ways these conversations served as a vehicle for reproducing or transforming their perceptions surrounding menopause and work during a second one-to-one interview (average length 34 minutes).

The decision to focus on young men about to join the labour market was two-fold. On the one hand, as graduates, they would soon be entering a labour market where leadership positions remain the domain of white men like themselves. On the other hand, they had been in full-time education during a time when talk of allyship had become mainstreamed in part due to the #MeToo and #BlackLivesMatter movements. As such, they may be at least more aware of ideas surrounding collective responsibilities to challenge dominant or oppressive structures. And while Gannon and Ekstrom suggested back in 1993 that young men are likely to be less familiar with and have less developed perceptions of menopause than other groups, knowledge of reproductive lives has been increasing for both young men and women in the UK at least. This is in part due to increased media coverage, such as UK TV celebrity Davina McCall's documentary 'Sex, myths and the menopause' and policy discussions, including the UK government's Menopause All-Party Parliamentary Group. Moreover, given the increasing average age of childbirth in the UK during the period this cohort was born, mothers of men in the age bracket of our participants are likely to be of menopausal or peri-menopausal age and thus have valuable insights and experiences to share. All participants also had experience of paid work, either through part-time employment or summer internships.

During the interviews, we sought to explore their understanding and perceptions of the menopause, their relationship to menopause and work and their role in a menopause supporting workplace. As a research team, we also discussed how to carefully frame the role of their discussion with their parent during fieldwork. For example, we had a lot of discussion about the problems of reproducing an inadvertent assumption of the 'mother's job' being to educate others about menopause. We sought to make sure in all interactions that we were clear that we were not suggesting that mothers should shoulder the burden for talking to their sons about menopause (any more than fathers should) and acquiesce to tired tropes of maternal failure. Institutional ethical approval was granted, while the research team also reflected on some of the ethical tensions that surfaced through the research design and data collection. For example, we discussed whether the research design had inadvertently suggested that respondents should seek knowledge or advice from older women in the workplace, reproducing the trope of the 'mothering manager' (Cutcher, 2021).

To facilitate analysis, all 12 interviews were transcribed by an external professional transcription company, anonymized and uploaded to NVivo12. The analysis involved two stages. The first stage was coding each transcript thematically to explore what ideas, perceptions or expectations surrounding menopause and allyship emerged, as well as other themes to come out inductively from the interviews: 138 codes emerged. Next, similar codes were organized into categories, generating 14 broad categories with sub-categories, often through different first order codes being distilled or combined. For example, the broad category 'understandings of menopause' consisted of sub-categories such as 'challenges of menopause', 'biological definitions' and 'trivialized menopause'. The second stage involved exploring the patterns between the different categories, assessing the degree of interdependency or distance between categories. Here we explored how ideas surrounding self-identity often appeared in close or overlapping extracts surrounding reasons for allyship. This stage allowed for a deeper dive into what different ideas were supporting or complementary, and likewise, which ones seemed juxtaposed or in contradistinction with each other. The findings are structured into three final themes: the starting point; being that 'someone else'; and generational masculinities.

Findings

The starting point

> 'I don't have a clue ... what [menopause] is, other than from conversations ... I've had with my mum. ... Other than that ... my knowledge of menopause is very minimal' (Frankie).

By their own admission, our respondents had very little understanding of menopause, and referred to a patchwork of sources that informed what they did know. Some referred to knowing about menopause via 'popular culture, you know, if it's in, like, films or TV ... I don't think anyone ever sat me down and went through it or taught it' (Chris), or through 'informal, general knowledge' (Tyler). Others discussed secondary school such as 'GCSE biology' (Martin) which followed a basic, biologically determined understanding. Martin went on to suggest that: 'I feel like society is becoming more accepting and discussions about menstruation are becoming more mainstream ... I think it's becoming part of ... sort of culture as well, whereby, I don't know, you'll have the sort of female comedians being willing to talk about it and broach it.'

Some young men attributed the absence of talk about menopause to cultural or systemic factors:

'Some people might be quite open to talking about [menopause], but I suppose as well in this country, maybe more so than like America and stuff, we're kind of more private about, like, our own bodies.' (Chris)

'I think that the existence of the stigma [surrounding menopause] ... is from long internalized patriarchal superstructures. ... So I think it's heavily ingrained in the DNA of hierarchies in the western world at least.' (Allan)

At the same time, all were very clear on why menopause was an issue relevant to workplaces and on the importance of raising awareness by all of those that work. Allan emphasized that such awareness raising itself was important in helping employees and managers understand how menopause is an important 'human issue': 'Learning about these issues is learning about human issues, you know, it, learning about how the other side works, it shouldn't even be like learning how the other side works. It's just learning how we work and so, with the sort of normalization of that kind of attitude.'

In justifying menopause as a workplace concern, respondents simultaneously upheld a rational 'business case' approach, and a more human-centred justification where 'it's just the decent thing to do, ehh, you know, sort of as humans' (Martin). Martin continued by saying: 'I think definitely, I think that the, the world is waking up to the fact that women, there's a massive untapped source of sort of growth, economic growth and massive benefits for companies that help women through this'.

Tyler recognized these two justifications were likely to exist simultaneously within organizational practice: 'I might be cynical, but a company is only going to address an issue when it helps their bottom line, so I don't know how you would incentivize [menopause support] without just sort of asking people to be nicer or more inclusive.'

However, recognition of menopause as a legitimate workplace issue often contrasted with a desire to 'place' menopause within particular workplace practices, cultures and experiences. And here a tension was identified by respondents who explained that where to begin understanding menopausal transition was felt as not having a 'home'. For example, Frankie emphasized that there seemed to be nowhere or no time to learn about menopause:

'The education that we got through school was all about what's happening there and then, and just, there was no preparation about what's happened, what, what happens in the future. So the education part from, is just lost when you go out of school because there's no, there's no like formal place to kind of prescribe that education on what [it] actually is.'

This sentiment of menopause having no location for a starting conversation after school came up in relation to workplaces, and was connected to not knowing where organizations might 'place' it. However, in considering this, respondents stressed the importance of recognizing that menopause was both heavily stigmatized and a 'way more nuanced issue than just "this is the biological effects"'(Allan), where 'it's not as binary as like a broken bone, whereby sort of, it's evident and it's either healing or not healing or it's broken or not broken' (Martin). Associated with this reasoning, some young men who Hannah interviewed aligned menopause with how (mental) health at work was positioned:

'Maybe actually if there's a culture of like openness about talking about health in general in a company, then that might you know, it might, if you put all the emphasis on the menopause itself that might make it less comfortable. But if it was just under the broad heading of health and you know everybody talks about their health and issues with their health, then that might be easier for them to talk.' (Chris)

'It might come under the same umbrella of dealing with mental health issues, something that's semi-behind the scenes, maybe more behind the scenes for some people. Ehh, which is something that could easily be brushed under the carpet.' (Tyler)

In sum, this opening theme highlighted key aspects of respondents' starting points for understanding menopause, and its relation to work. While formal secondary education provided some with a biological frame for understanding menopause, all noted the historical silence about menstrual issues within western societies that is changing with greater public awareness. That said, beyond attributing a general importance to supporting menopausal transition to human capital arguments or broader notions of social justice, there were difficulties in imagining a starting point for conversations about menopause at work among respondents. This suggested a lack of a clear discursive position from which respondents felt confident to develop or express knowledge about the subject.

Being that 'someone else'

'It's not enough to just *think* that something isn't right ... you've got to follow up and be that person that says something' (Chris).

The next theme central to our respondents' accounts was the importance of being the person that did something, said something, or took responsibility for their own learning, rather than being a bystander or accepting their lack of knowledge. In speaking to this, our respondents emphasized the/their role of/as men in reproducing and/or challenging menopause-related stigma in organizational settings.

Like others, Tyler suggested that it is 'impossible to discount the impact that men have', both on changing social attitudes to menopause and supporting menopausal transition in the workplace. For some, this influence took the form of reproducing stigmatizing or negating comments. For example, speaking to their mothers' accounts of being ignored or ridiculed was central in some respondents' talk about how they became aware of needing to adopt a more proactive stance to counter stigmatized or marginalizing cultures surrounding menopause at work. In Chris's case, for instance, this meant an emergent understanding that he needed to be a person who did not ignore stigmatizing cultures or was a bystander:

'I was just unaware of how unsupportive some people can be of it due to lack of understanding, due to not having conversations and stuff like that and, eh, and yeah just people not wanting to understand it, or trying to ignore that somebody is dealing with it.'

While recognizing that men are more likely to occupy influential positions in organizations, there was a lack of consensus among the respondents over what they should do in these positions. Some found it difficult to balance recognizing current gendered systems of dominance in the workplace with considering what men should do. This was exemplified in Martin's account which referred to women 'fulfilling potential':

'I feel like, that's sort of the way that it, sort of the way you're looking at it about men empowering women in terms of being able to bring them up and sort of fulfil their potential because, unfortunately, it is the case that they are a sort of higher concentration at senior levels.'

By comparison, Allan recognized the ambivalence involved in men using their workplace position to challenge power relations, even if it might come across as tokenistic or 'shallow' in some ways:

'If someone in a position of, a man in a position of power with the, in a position where he's able to influence structural change to what, to whatever extent … then this is just a tool to use, for, you know … it's probably necessary in a lot of ways to, to use these men in that way … engage in their help, or whatever, even if it's sort of shallow.'

At the same time, there was a clear recognition that it is not just acknowledging the lived experience of menopausal women as valuable, but that the act of listening is vital:

'It's difficult to understand things if you don't talk to someone who's went through the experience. It's like erm, you know white people can talk about race all day but if you don't speak to someone who's actually had, been like affected by it, it's kind of difficult to fully understand it. And it's like about having the ability to listen to people that's been affected, even if you're not going to go through it yourself but to be able to empathize and, you know, have empathy with people about it.' (Chris)

Allan went further by suggesting 'you know, I can't relate, but I can't just displace it'.

In all, this second theme drew attention to respondents' recognition of the/their need to be that 'someone' that does or says something to counteract menopause-related stigma in social interactions and to consider how to use any authority or power in future workplace settings to that end. Their responses express a lack of consensus, however, on what that might look like in practice.

Generational masculinities

When undertaking the interviews, Hannah reflected that 'they are young men. A lot of what they are about is about being young men'. In many ways, this side comment spoke to the myriad of ways that the respondents' articulation of supporting menopausal transition in the workplace was intimately situated in their own identities as young men. For some, this manifested in a socially felt acceptance of their ignorance surrounding menopause. For example, Martin suggests he is 'age-ranged' out of discussion and awareness:

'I think with menopause ... I don't feel like it's part of mainstream discussion yet ... or at least it doesn't feed down to a male in his 20s, which I am, and I feel like maybe part of that is because there's still – I reckon – some taboo that has sort of hung around from that [older] generation ... I feel like also ... there's an age gap between sort of my age and anyone who has sort of been experiencing it and there's also a gender gap as well that exists whereby I mean ... men obviously don't menstruate.'

Similarly, Chris suggested that 'no one has felt the need to, like, explain it to me', amidst a general consensus that menopausal stigma was due to 'male perception not being great' (Frankie). For some, such perceptions served to displace responsibility for self-education, suggesting that menopausal understanding needed to be 'brought to them' through formal training. Other respondents, however, were aware of taking ownership over (their own) proactive behaviours. The motivation to do so was often set up through generational comparisons between themselves and an 'old guard' of male managers or style of management:

'I do feel like there's a generational thing with the older men whereby [menopause] was never part of the mainstream conversation. It was all very, always very taboo. I'm not saying that the younger generation is sort of incredibly well-informed but I do feel like there are large barriers in terms of understanding and also acceptance … with that generation.' (Martin)

'I remember my boss over summer was like ex-military … he wasn't, like, strict but he had that very masculine, classical manager kind of vibe. I think that would pose more challenges [to open communication] than someone who was more open-minded, not open-minded, more communicative and more in touch with their employees or people they work with than someone who takes a more hierarchical role.' (Tyler)

Tyler continued to talk about how young people in general may be more open to discussion:

'I think people of my age are more willing to just talk about anything. I don't know of many subjects that hold the same stigma, that you see, in older generations, that I have seen in older generations, and things that just wouldn't get addressed. Whereas, in my experience of people who are my peers or people at uni[versity], there are few things which have been stigmatized.'

At the same time, some of the dynamics in the interviews and accounts of the discussions with their mums did suggest that there was also a lingering hesitance that emerged around what should be discussed vis-à-vis what they wanted to be seen to discuss. In particular, this may be highly contextual for the young men we interviewed. That is to say, they might be happy to discuss menopause with certain people in certain spaces, but not with other people or in other spaces. In this sense, 'stigma' appeared to manifest in more subtle forms, through, for example, 'preferring not' to like certain comments on social media, or not being able to imagine scenarios when the topic might 'come up' when talking to peers or future work colleagues. Their preferences speak to a complex negotiation that was framed as choosing to engage or not, and how this might happen, in the spaces of interaction where they expect to perform more normative masculine identities (through, for example, talking about sport).

Concluding discussion
The (im)possibilities of menopausal allyship?

Moving from the interview findings, this section discusses what we can learn from these young men hoping to embark on a future career in a managerial position in a white collar professional setting in terms of the possibilities of male allyship for educating about, advocating for and supporting menopausal transition at work as a form of gender or menopausal equality. While we make no claims of generalizability from this small and somewhat self-selecting group, this study does provide an insight into those who are perhaps likely to be amenable to allyship (in principle). On a positive note, we found that there was an open acceptance that menopause at work was a legitimate area for organizational support, and that it was understood not simply as a biological issue but also impacted by cultural stigma. We were also encouraged by the young men's reflections that their lack of understanding around menopause was not good enough and that they felt a responsibility for knowing, even if they did not articulate complete ownership of being responsible for educating themselves. But these general findings belie further layers of complexity characterized by tensions and ambivalences in the young men's accounts of male allyship for menopause. These tensions may be viewed, for instance, in:

- The desire to construct allyship subjectivities as emerging from a position of knowledge about a given subject, but at the same time acknowledging they do not know much about an idea/experience they cannot see or apprehend and can at best approximate in terms of mental health challenges (rather than the menopause experience as a whole). This may feed into limited ways of talking about or making visible menopause at work. At a conceptual level, this may also demand the impossible – a monolithically intelligible menopausal subject position – in order for others to come to know and recognize menopause.

- Uncertainty about the 'ownership' of responsibility for education, and the broader responsibility of organizations for training and support. This appears to rest upon an accumulation of institutionally sanctioned ignorance where a lack of reference during school education sets expectations about where and how menopause should be introduced and discussed.
- The relational nesting of masculinity and age as points of reference for the young men to both understand the potential of being male allies for menopause, and to negate understanding of the potential/challenges of such allyship. This notes the subjective potential and agency for allyship as age- and gender-situated, but this positionality also brings about different ambivalences about how, and where, to publicly acknowledge and engage with menopause as an issue of workplace inequality.

Though in a different context, these tensions echo the experiences reflected upon by Tienari and Taylor (2019). That is to say, on the one hand, the interview findings demonstrate a range of different positions that men hold in relation to their perceived future capacity or capability to effect gender equality in respect of menopausal support at work. And on the other, these different positions are also linked relationally to their own gendered identity beliefs and practices.

Such a challenge speaks to the broader tensions of advocating for allyship and organizations. In particular, there exists an ongoing tension between allies taking responsibility for their own actions and practices of allyship, while also suggesting that formal bodies (such as schools or organizations) need to play a role in education and awareness. While both individual and cultural aspects are vital for allyship work, there is also a danger that individuals view allyship as an accoutrement to working life without appreciating the full implications and responsibility that it brings. This may lead to criticism of workplace allyship practices that do not view challenge or disruption as necessary to effect change. This is similar to Sumerau et al's (2021, p 369) findings among college students who self-identified as allies and were focused on 'construct[ing] allyship as a way to both symbolically oppose inequalities while also avoiding taking any direct action toward challenging inequitable social systems'.

Our findings also echo previous research by Nash et al (2021, p 13) which showed that 'men are more likely to become champions of change if they are aware of gender bias, believe that gender equality is worthwhile, are inclined to defy some masculine gender norms, and are committed to helping others'. However, we additionally highlight that the intersection between gender and youthful subject positions is central to how our respondents sought to situate themselves as potential menopause allies. In some ways youthful masculinities appeared to mitigate some of the difficulties of engaging with what Casey (2010, p 267) called '"average" men'. In her study of allyship and sexual violence, Casey identifies the continual challenge posed by men who do not see the focus of allyship as something directly relevant to their lives. In response to this, we would say our findings suggest that it is vital to have a nuanced understanding of and response to allies' positionalities. In our study this also helped to better understand allyship as not simply moving against gendered inequality, but also against more normative or traditional modes of masculinity that were attached to older cohorts in the workforce. Of course, this no doubt also interlaces with class and socio-economic dynamics given that the six men we spoke to were university educated and relatively privileged. Their accounts of their relationship with menopause as a topic thus align with contemporary modalities of youthful masculinities that bring together new masculinities (Messerschmidt and Messner, 2018) with the concept of youthful subjectivities (McRobbie, 2002) as embodying a particular agential power to evoke change.

Of course, we are also aware that there may be other challenges in male menopausal allyships which rely upon supplanting one mode of masculinity for another, such as 'democratic' or 'empathic' manhood (Kimmel, 2017). However well intentioned, this may not challenge the existing gendered dualisms upon which much of the sexist discourses surrounding menopause rest. At worst, it may slip into a discussion of relations between men and women that reproduce the idea of women as requiring help from men, even though accounts elsewhere suggest that a majority of women successfully negotiate menopausal transition at work by themselves (Jack, Riach and Bariola, 2019). Or it may result in men expecting the gift of 'the gratitude of women' that de Vries (2015, p 29) suggests. In such cases, it may indeed be that for men, 'doing nothing is sometimes better' (Bishop, 2002, p 127).

As such, while allyship might provide a useful term that is recognized in the workplace due to its mainstreaming into society, it is unclear just yet whether the way it is understood or currently appropriated in the workplace may serve to radically alter or transform organizations towards inclusive menopausal cultures and contribute to gender equality. However, given we know that 'despite the difficulty many men experience in noticing sexism, they are particularly effective when they do speak up about sexism' (Drury and Kaiser, 2014, p 649), we would suggest closer attention to practices that may sit alongside, develop, or go beyond allyship practices that bring men into conversations about menopause and the workplace.

References

Anicha, C. L., Burnett, A. and Bilen-Green, C. (2015) 'Men faculty gender-equity advocates: a qualitative analysis of theory and praxis', *The Journal of Men's Studies*, 23(1): 21–43.

Atcheson, S. (2018) 'Allyship – the key to unlocking the power of diversity', *Forbes*, [online], Available from: https://www.forbes.com/sites/shereeatche son/2018/11/30/allyship-the-key-to-unlocking-the-power-of-diversity/ ?sh=23551d1049c6 [Accessed 20 April 2022].

Atkinson, C., Beck, V., Brewis, J., Davies, A. and Duberley, J. (2021a) 'Menopause and the workplace: New directions in HRM research and HR practice', *Human Resource Management Journal*, 31(1): 49–64.

Atkinson, C., Carmichael, F. and Duberley, J. (2021b) 'The menopause taboo at work: Examining women's embodied experiences of menopause in the UK police service', *Work, Employment and Society*, 35(4): 657–76.

Beck, V., Brewis, J. and Davies, A. (2020) 'The remains of the taboo: Experiences, attitudes, and knowledge about menopause in the workplace', *Climacteric,* 23(2): 158–64.

Bishop, A. (2002) *Becoming an Ally: Breaking the Cycle of Oppression in People* (2nd edn), Halifax, Canada: Fernwood Publishing.

Bloomberg (2022) 'Confronting the taboo surrounding menopause in the workplace', [online], 28 January, Available from: https://www.bloomb erg.com/company/stories/confronting-the-taboo-surrounding-menopa use-in-the-workplace/ [Accessed 20 April 2022].

Butler, C. (2020) 'Managing the menopause through "abjection work": When boobs can become embarrassingly useful, again', *Work, Employment and Society*, 34(4): 696–712.

Caçapava Rodolpho, J.R., Cid Quirino, B., Komura Hoga, L.A. and Lima Ferreira Santa Rosa, P. (2016) 'Men's perceptions and attitudes toward their wives experiencing menopause', *Journal of Women & Aging*, 28(4): 322–33.

Casey, E. (2010) 'Strategies for engaging men as anti-violence allies: Implications for ally movements', *Advances in Social Work*, 11(2): 267–82.

Corbett, H. (2020) '6 ways to be an authentic ally at work', *Forbes*, [online], 24 January, Available from: https://www.forbes.com/sites/hollycorbett/2022/01/24/6-ways-to-be-an-authentic-ally-at-work/?sh=114e17ae70dd [Accessed 28 June 2022].

Cutcher, L. (2021) 'Mothering managers: (Re)interpreting older women's organisational subjectivity', *Gender, Work and Organization*, 28(4): 1447–60.

De Vries, J.A. (2015) 'Champions of gender equality: Female and male executives as leaders of gender change', *Equality, Diversity and Inclusion: An International Journal*, 34(1): 21–36.

Drury, B.J. and Kaiser, C.R. (2014) 'Allies against sexism: The role of men in confronting sexism', *Journal of Social Issues*, 70(4): 637–52.

Gannon, L. and Ekstrom, B. (1993) 'Attitudes toward menopause: The influence of sociocultural paradigms', *Psychology of Women Quarterly*, 17(3): 275–88.

Hardy, C., Griffiths, A. and Hunter, M.S. (2019) 'Development and evaluation of online menopause awareness training for line managers in UK organizations', *Maturitas*, 120: 83–9.

Hidiroglu, S., Tanriover, O., Ay, P. and Karavus, M. (2014) 'A qualitative study on menopause described from the man's perspective', *Journal of Pakistan Medical Association*, 64(9): 1031–6.

Jack, G., Riach, K., Bariola, E., Pitts, M., Schapper, J. and Sarrel, P. (2016) 'Menopause in the workplace: What employers should be doing', *Maturitas*, 85, 88–95.

Jack, G., Riach, K. and Bariola, E. (2019) 'Temporality and gendered agency: Menopausal subjectivities in women's work', *Human Relations*, 72(1): 122–43.

Johnson, W.B. and Smith, D.G. (2018) 'How men can become better allies to women', *Harvard Business Review*, [online], 12 October, Available from: https://hbr.org/2018/10/how-men-can-become-better-allies-to-women [Accessed 28 June 2022].

Kelan, E.K. (2018) 'Men doing and undoing gender at work: A review and research agenda', *International Journal of Management Reviews*, 20(2): 544–58.

Kelan, E.K. and Wratil, P. (2018) 'Post-heroic leadership, tempered radicalism and senior leaders as change agents for gender equality', *European Management Review*, 15(1): 5–18.

Kimmel, M. (2017) *Manhood in America*, New York: Oxford University Press.

Lansu, M., Bleijenbergh, I. and Benschop, Y. (2020) 'Just talking? Middle managers negotiating problem ownership in gender equality interventions', *Scandinavian Journal of Management*, 36(2): 101–10.

Lorbiecki, A. and Jack, G. (2000) 'Critical turns in the evolution of diversity management', *British Journal of Management*, 11(s1): S17–S31.

Madsen, S.R., Townsend, A. and Scribner, R.T. (2020) 'Strategies that male allies use to advance women in the workplace', *The Journal of Men's Studies*, 28(3): 239–59.

Mavin, S. (2008) 'Queen bees, wannabees and afraid to bees: No more "best enemies" for women in management?', *British Journal of Management*, 19(s1): S75–S84.

McRobbie, A. (2002) 'Different, youthful, subjectivities', in I. Chambers and L. Curti (eds) *The Postcolonial Question: Common Skies, Divided Horizons*, London: Routledge, pp 40–56.

Melaku, T.M., Beeman, A., Smith, D.G. and Johnson, W.B. (2020) 'Be a better ally', *Harvard Business Review*, 98(6): 135–9.

Messerschmidt, J.W. and Messner, M.A. (2018) 'Hegemonic, nonhegemonic, and "new" masculinities', in J.W. Messerschmidt, M.A. Messner, R. Connell and P. Yancey Martin (eds) *Gender Reckonings: New Social Theory and Research*, New York: New York University Press, pp 35–56.

Nash, M., Grant, R., Moore, R. and Winzenberg, T. (2021) 'Male allyship in institutional STEMM gender equity initiatives', *PLOS ONE*, 16(3): e0248373.

Parish, S.J., Faubion, S.S., Weinberg, M., Bernick, B. and Mirkin, S. (2019) 'The MATE survey: Men's perceptions and attitudes towards menopause and their role in partners' menopausal transition', *Menopause*, 26(10): 1110–6.

Riach, K., Loretto, W. and Krekula, C. (2015) 'Gendered ageing in the new economy: Introduction to special issue', *Gender, Work & Organization*, 22(5): 437–44.

Riach, K. and Jack, G. (2021) 'Women's health in/and work: Menopause as an intersectional experience', *International Journal of Environmental Research and Public Health*, 18(20): 10793.

Sawyer, K. and Valerio, A.M. (2018) 'Making the case for male champions for gender inclusiveness at work', *Organizational Dynamics*, 47(1): 1–7.

Steffan, B. and Potočnik, K. (2023) 'Thinking outside Pandora's Box: Revealing differential effects of coping with physical and psychological menopause symptoms at work', *Human Relations*, 76(8): 1191–1225.

Sumerau, J., Forbes, T.D., Grollman, E.A. and Mathers, L.A. (2021) 'Constructing allyship and the persistence of inequality', *Social Problems*, 68(2): 358–73.

The Law Society (2018) 'Male champions for change toolkit', [online], 17 March, Available from: https://www.lawsociety.org.uk/en/campaigns/women-in-leadership-in-law/tools/male-champions-for-change-tool kit#:~:text=One%20of%20the%20Law%20Society's,play%20in%20achiev ing%20gender%20balance [Accessed 20 April 2022].

Tienari, J. and Taylor, S. (2019) 'Feminism and men: Ambivalent space for acting up', *Organization*, 26(6): 948–60.

Where Women Work (2022) '#BreakTheBias around menopause in the workplace', [online], 3 March, Available from: https://www.wherewomenw ork.com/Career/4183/Menopause-workplace-allyship [Accessed 20 April].

Zhang, X., Wang, G., Wang, H., Wang, X., Ji, T., Hou, D., Wu, J., Sun, J. and Zhu, B. (2020) 'Spouses' perceptions of and attitudes toward female menopause: A mixed-methods systematic review', *Climacteric*, 23(2): 148–57.

8

Conclusion

Vanessa Beck and Jo Brewis

In this short editorial conclusion, we draw out the key messages offered throughout the volume's chapters, highlighting areas where these chapters complement each other and/or make contributions to the knowledge base on menopause transitions and the workplace. This foundation is then used to re-assess areas which require further development, or which have opened up as new research areas given the now expanded knowledge base. This culminates in a clear research agenda to follow going forwards as we hope to see menopause transitions in the workplace becoming a more established research field.

Our edited volume has brought together chapters covering menopause as a biopsychosocial process; transitions within workplaces; flexible working; trade unions, the spatial context of work; and male allyship in organizations. With this breadth of subject matter, we have made clear contributions and advanced knowledge on menopause in the following, important ways. First, the chapters have helped counter the still predominantly biomedical discourse around menopause and have furthered the discussions around a biopsychosocial approach. Karen Throsby and Celia Roberts do this most prominently in Chapter 2, and set the tone for the whole volume thereby. As their analysis makes clear, although the provision of HRT is an important subject and the focus on the availability of such medication in UK parliamentary activities is welcome (All-Party Parliamentary Group on Menopause, 2022; Women and Equalities Committee, 2022), there is a need for an extension of support for menopausal women to consider social and cultural factors. We also need, as Karen and Celia establish, to open up the conversation around menopause to include those who are often excluded – LGBTQI+ people, people with disabilities, people who do not have children and those who go through premature menopause – in workplaces and elsewhere.

Equally, public discussions around menopause have increased awareness, yet knowledge about how best to practically implement knowledge and make a difference in families, social settings and workplaces – our focus here – is still underdeveloped. Practice is in fact running considerably ahead of research here, and as such academic assessments of menopause interventions in organizations are still very much needed. Jane Parry's analysis of flexible work in Chapter 3 is therefore an important addition to the knowledge base. The chapters have made a second contribution in this practical arena by expanding the analysis of how workplaces can and should address menopause issues. It is clear that a menopause policy or guidelines by themselves are insufficient to make meaningful change but that much can be achieved by already established policies, practices and regulations, such as the right to request flexible working.

While such structures require adjustments to make them more broadly available and suitable for the range of menopause experiences, as Jane avers, simultaneously working towards cultural change in organizations could provide meaningful support. Instilling a positive sense of community, and with that creating a psychological contract that works for both employees and employers, produces a situation with enhanced possibilities for those transitioning through menopause and for organizational aims and objectives overall. Using the concept of a psychological contract, as Carol Atkinson, Jo Duberley and Catrina Page do in Chapter 4, highlights two important considerations. Most obviously this is about the relationship between workers and management and attempts to build positive relationships that are mutually beneficial. A flip side to this is that the cultural and structural changes required in workplaces cannot be undertaken unilaterally, hence the need for a more or less implicit contract that specifies roles and responsibilities for all participants in the workplace. The important role that trade unions have already played in addressing menopause in the workplace can be made a part of a desired cultural change, in particular as they have the future potential to provide support via trade union representatives and training structures, as Vanessa establishes in Chapter 5.

Third, the chapters have made meaningful suggestions to address perennial problems in workplaces, including the issues of temperature regulation and mutual support. Considerations of spatial justice, as provided by Jo in Chapter 6, are an innovative way to address the often-raised problems of varying preferences for temperature regulation in workplaces, which are frequently heightened for individuals transitioning through menopause. More broadly speaking, workplaces have to accommodate different needs and requirements and the spatial justice approach provides a foundation for equitable and fair ways to do this.

To achieve this, mutual understanding and support is again key and, although this goes far beyond gender differences, cis male allyship for those experiencing menopause transition is an important starting point. Ideas of allyship and solidarity as a means to improve support, discussed by Hannah Bardett, Kathleen Riach and Gavin Jack in Chapter 7, are also a way to ensure the development of the psychological contract mentioned earlier. Whether allyship is founded on gender, and solidarity is between trade union members or between workers sharing workspaces, the basic principle is that the more people are on board, the easier it will be for those transitioning through menopause, and the more likely it is that organizational, cultural and structural changes can be made to ensure that support is available. Such solidarity can also ensure that the improvements made in workplaces will benefit everybody experiencing menopause transition and can also lead to improvements for the workforce overall. This is an important point as many of the interventions which are helpful for menopausal staff will also help their colleagues – for example, those with any of the conditions which might increase sensitivity to high temperatures (Brewis, this volume, Chapter 6).

Nonetheless, despite the highlighted achievements made via the individual chapters, and the parallel contributions to our knowledge on menopause at work, it is still the case that there is a long way to go for both workplace practice and academic research, as we argued in our introduction. It is important not to be complacent because there are still many cis women and other employees out there struggling with their menopause symptoms at and because of work. Emerging out of the contributions made in this volume, we therefore suggest an agenda of issues below that are in need of further academic investigation, empirical research, and/or policy and workplace practice development.

Before we do so, we should first of all reiterate that both research and practice have made considerable strides over the last few years. There were very few empirical studies reporting UK data in terms of menopause and its connections to work just five years ago, as we discovered when we were compiling our report for the Government

Equalities Office (Brewis et al, 2017). We now have a better grasp on the specificities of UK workplaces, occupations and economic sectors in this respect, including via the contributions to this volume.

Many UK organizations have also introduced workplace interventions around menopause in recent times, as the range of case studies at Henpicked: Menopause in the Workplace (nd) and the growing list of employers who have either been accredited as menopause friendly or have committed to this endeavour (The Menopause Friendly Accreditation, nd) suggest. Internal evaluations in these organizations point to the initiatives being very well received, as do the studies published by Hardy et al (2018a; Hardy, Griffiths and Hunter 2019a) and Verburgh et al (2020). Yet while we understand more about how such interventions take effect and the impact of policies and practices on employees' experiences of menopause, the evidence base remains incomplete. Further research is required here on a broader range of organizations and settings to explore the specifics of different types of policies and guidelines and how they may result (or not) in actual changes for the practices and cultures in workplaces.

We have also learned more about the perspective of mid-life cis women themselves. In their voices, it has been made clear that there are feelings of being judged negatively by colleagues, managers and clients/customers/end users on the basis of menopausal symptoms and that women often feel stereotyped as being 'of a certain age'. As a result, a common theme is that women are reluctant to disclose their menopause experiences. However, we still have less evidence about how line managers and colleagues feel or would react. And there is also a need for further research from any location on how menopause symptoms might affect the ability to look for or secure work, working hours, remuneration, career development, decisions to remain at or leave work, being made redundant, being performance managed or being dismissed.

Moreover, and as we suggested in an article in *HRMJ* (Atkinson et al, 2021), we still know almost nothing about workplace menopause transitions in terms of intersectionality – for example, women who do not have children (whether electively or not), women with disabilities, BAME women, women of different religions, women who identify as lesbian or bisexual and those who identify as transgender, non-binary or gender nonconforming. This is of course something that Karen and Celia also establish in Chapter 2. This lack of knowledge also includes the range of employment sectors and working experiences.

In 2017, Office of National Statistics data showed that more than half of women in paid employment in the UK are in occupations classified as non-managerial, nonprofessional or non-technical, all of which are still under-represented in menopause research. Kathleen and Gavin have written about the intersectional connections between gender, age, health and work demands in the experiences of menopausal staff elsewhere, and their respondents were employed in a wide range of occupations in higher education and healthcare (Riach and Jack, 2021). Verburgh et al (2020), who we also cited in our introduction, focus on women in low-paid jobs. However, these studies are unusual in the wider field of menopause at work research.

We also lack understanding of the experiences of mid-life women in occupations or sectors where regulations – around uniforms, say – or working arrangements like zero hours contracts can make it challenging for them to request adjustments to their workplace environments or ask for flexible working. On this last, Yoeli, Macnaughton and McLusky (2021) have – again as we noted earlier – undertaken a meta-review of research on menopausal women in precarious work. Revealingly, despite a concentrated effort to locate studies of this kind, they found only 13.

Similar to the lack of intersectional analysis, comparative combinations of perspectives and experiences are scarce. As we also established in our *HRMJ* article (Atkinson et al, 2021), there are no studies of menopause experiences in workplaces across different countries or studies directly comparing the experiences of mid-life women and mid-life men at work. The latter makes it difficult to disentangle mid-life experiences at work generally from those unique to menopause. Moreover, the extant literature focuses – in many ways quite rightly – on the difficult situations that those experiencing menopause transition face in the workplace. But this results in an evidence base that paints an overwhelmingly negative picture of the experience of menopause at work, with honourable exceptions including Jack, Riach and Bariola (2019) and Butler (2020), again as cited in our introduction. As such, we need to understand more about neutral or even positive experiences to put a comprehensive picture in place. One reason why this is important is that younger individuals who are trying to learn about menopause as something they and/or their colleagues, families and friends will encounter in the future should not only expect difficult and negative experiences, something which could well make them apprehensive or scared.

Other persistent evidence gaps include: a lack of HR perspectives; few studies using anything other than self-report mechanisms to capture menopause symptoms and/or work performance; and no studies which comprehensively quantify the economic costs of menopause symptoms. Although Evandrou et al (2021) and Bryson et al (2022) have produced very important work around women leaving work or reducing their hours due to struggling with their symptoms, their data do not allow them to quantify the associated costs for either the women themselves or their employers. We still need to understand more about both the extensive and intensive margins of costs, including those borne by employers, workers' families and wider society.

In the UK specifically, we have also been very disappointed by the government's response to reports from the Women and Equalities Committee (WEC, 2022) and the All-Party Parliamentary Group on Menopause (APPGM, 2022) reports. WEC, to whom the government were obliged to respond, made 17 separate recommendations, including eight which focused on the workplace and associated employment rights legislation. These included:

- The creation of the post of national Menopause Ambassador;
- The right to request flexible working arrangements, as discussed by Jane Parry in Chapter 3, to start from the first day of someone's employment;
- The enactment of Section 14 of the Equality Act 2010 to broaden the basis on which dual claims of discrimination can be brought – for example, using sex and age for this purpose;
- Adding menopause as a protected characteristic to the same Act, mirroring the status which pregnancy and maternity already have;
- Developing 'model' menopause policies as guidance for employers; and
- Working with a major public sector employer to evaluate the likely efficacy of a policy on menopause leave.

Only the first two recommendations were accepted when the government's response was finally published on the 18 January 2023, almost four months late (UK Government, 2023). As UK Parliament (nd) documentation suggests, the usual period for a written response to a Select Committee report is 60 days. Indeed the same documentation states that the response to the WEC report was due on 28 September 2022. It is also worth noting that the government had already pledged to enact the recommendation around the right to request flexible working patterns in December 2022.

Jo has written about the government response separately (Brewis, 2023); and we have also detailed why we think the rejection of menopause leave is problematic in more depth in another piece (Brewis and Beck, 2023). And we were not altogether surprised by what the government had to say, given that the Department of Work and Pensions (DWP, 2022) had already turned down similar recommendations made in an independent report on menopause as a workplace issue, commissioned by the Minster for Employment, including menopause becoming a protected characteristic. This was compiled by the 50 Plus Choices Employer Taskforce (5PCET, 2021), which is chaired by the Government's Business Champion for the Ageing Society and Older Worker and includes representatives from bodies like Business in the Community and the Chartered Institute for Personnel and Development.

The APPGM report (2022: 13) made two key recommendations about menopause in the workplace, as follows:

- The government must co-ordinate and support an employer-led campaign to raise awareness of menopause in the workplace and to help tackle the taboo surrounding menopause and work. This campaign must promote the importance of supporting employees through the menopause transition as a core employee health issue, and promote the business case for investing in employee support.
- The government must update and promote guidance for employers on best practice menopause at work policies and supporting interventions. This should include the economic justification and productivity benefits of doing so and be tailored to organizations of different sizes and resources to ensure it is as effective as possible.

As APPGs are not formally constituted committees, no government response to the APPGM report is mandated. Instead the hope would be to influence policy via collaborations with government departments like Health and Social Care. However, given that they refused to accept the very similar WEC (2022) recommendation around model menopause policies, it is clear that no progress will be made on this issue nor indeed on the first recommendation. It is also worth noting that the DWP (2022, np) reply to the 5PCET report, which contained a very similar recommendation around an employer-led campaign, was simply to state that 'We will use ... links with established partnerships and campaigns ... to increase the reach of menopause communications'. They added 'we will encourage the development of support within [employers'] organisations by providing links to advice, guidance and best practice case studies'. But we are not at all convinced that this equates to coordination of or support for 'an employer-led campaign'.

Given this tokenistic, piecemeal and unsatisfactory reaction from the UK government, at least thus far, to the persistent and pressing issue of menopause in the workplace, especially given the four cases we discussed in our introduction, the need for more research in this area as outlined in the foregoing seems yet more clear and present. As we suggested in our introduction, we hope that the arguments made here, and throughout this edited volume, will spur readers to undertake this scholarship, as well as to engage in menopause-related practice in their own workplaces.

References

50 Plus Choices Employer Taskforce (2021) *Menopause and Employment: How to Enable Fulfilling Working Lives*, [online], 25 November. Available from: https://www.thephoenixgroup.com/news-views/menopause-and-employment-how-to-enable-fulfilling-working-lives/ [Accessed 12 December 2022].

All-Party Parliamentary Group on Menopause (2022) *Inquiry to Assess the Impacts of Menopause and the Case for Policy Reform. Concluding Report*, [online], 12 October. Available from: https://menopause-appg.co.uk/wp-content/uploads/2022/10/APPG-Menopause-Inquiry-Concluding-Report-12.10.22-1.pdf [Accessed 17 November 2022].

Atkinson, C., Beck, V., Brewis, J., Davies, A. and Duberley, J. (2021) 'Menopause and the workplace: New directions in HRM research and HR practice', *Human Resource Management Journal*, 31(1): 49–64.

Brewis, J. (2023) 'The government may have rejected menopause protections – but workplaces are more supportive than ever', *The Conversation*, [online], 6 February. Available from: https://theconversation.com/the-uk-government-may-have-rejected-menopause-protections-but-workplaces-are-more-supportive-than-ever-198935 [Accessed 28 July 2023].

Brewis, J. and Beck, V. (2023) 'How to design menopause leave policies that really support women in the workplace', *The Conversation*, [online], 12 September. Available from: https://theconversation.com/how-to-design-menopause-leave-policies-that-really-support-women-in-the-workplace-209282 [Accessed 26 September 2023].

Brewis, J., Beck, V., Davies, A. and Matheson, J. (2017) *The Impact of Menopause Transition on Women's Economic Participation in the UK*, [online], 20 July. Available from: https://www.gov.uk/government/publications/menopause-transition-effects-on-womens-economic-participation [Accessed 17 November 2022].

Bryson, A., Conti, G., Hardy, G., Hardy, R., Peycheva, D. and Sullivan, A. (2022) 'The consequences of early menopause and menopause symptoms for labour market participation', *Social Science & Medicine*, 293, 114676.

Butler, C. (2020) 'Managing the menopause through "abjection work": When boobs can become embarrassingly useful, again', *Work, Employment and Society*, 34(4): 696–712.

Department of Work and Pensions (2022) *Policy Paper – Menopause and the Workplace: How to Enable Fulfilling Working Lives: Government Response*, [online], 25 November. Available from: https://www.gov.uk/government/publications/menopause-and-the-workplace-how-to-enable-fulfilling-working-lives-government-response/menopause-and-the-workplace-how-to-enable-fulfilling-working-lives-government-response [Accessed 12 December 2022].

Evandrou, M., Falkingham, J., Qin, M. and Vlachantoni, A. (2021) 'Menopausal transition and change in employment: Evidence from the National Child Development Study', *Maturitas*, 143(Jan): 96–104.

Hardy, C., Griffiths, A., Norton, S. and Hunter, M.S. (2018) 'Self-help cognitive behavior therapy for working women with problematic hot flushes and night sweats (MENOS@Work): A multicenter randomized controlled trial', *Menopause*, 25(5): 508–19.

Hardy, C., Griffiths, A. and Hunter, M. (2019) 'Development and evaluation of online menopause awareness training for line managers in UK organizations', *Maturitas*, 120(February): 83–9.

Henpicked: Menopause in the Workplace (nd) [online]. Available from: https://menopauseintheworkplace.co.uk/ [Accessed 12 December 2022].

Jack, G., Riach, K. and Bariola, E. (2019) 'Temporality and gendered agency: Menopausal subjectivities in women's work', *Human Relations*, 72(1): 122–43.

The Menopause Friendly Accreditation (nd) [online]. Available from: https://menopausefriendly.co.uk/ [Accessed 12 December 2022].

Riach, K. and Jack, G. (2021) 'Women's health in/and work: Menopause as an intersectional experience', *International Journal of Environmental Research and Public Health*, 18(20). doi: 10.3390/ijerph182010793.

UK Government (2023) *Menopause and the Workplace: Government Response to the Committee's First Report of Session 2022–2023 – Fourth Special Report of Session 2022–23*, [online], 18 January. Available from: https://committees. parliament.uk/publications/33631/documents/183795/default/ [Accessed 28 July 2023].

UK Parliament (nd) *Select Committees*, [online]. Available from: https://www. parliament.uk/about/how/committees/select/ [Accessed 12 December 2022].

Verburgh, M., Verdonk, P., Appelman, Y., Brood-van Zanten, M. and Nieuwenhuijsen, K. (2020) '"I get that spirit in me" – mentally empowering workplace health promotion for female workers in low-paid jobs during menopause and midlife', *International Journal of Environmental Research and Public Health*, 17(18), 6462.

Women and Equalities Committee (2022) *Menopause and the Workplace*, [online], 28 July. Available from: https://committees.parliament.uk/ work/1416/menopause-and-the-workplace/ [Accessed 17 November 2022].

Yoeli, H., Macnaughton, J. and McLusky, S. (2021) 'Menopausal symptoms and work: A narrative review of women's experiences in casual, informal, or precarious jobs', *Maturitas*, 150(August): 14–21.

Index

References to endnotes show both the page number and the note number (35n2).

menopause as workplace issue
  legitimate 145
menopause café 138
Menopause Friendly Accreditation 3, 4
menopause policy 76, 78
menopause symptoms 43
  reasonable adjustments for 58, 79
  severity and impact 47
Men's Attitudes Toward Menopause (MATE)
  study 136
mental health at work 145–6
Merchant vs BT (2012) 44
#MeToo 142
mid-life women 3, 4, 5–6, 23, 26, 27, 33,
  160, 161
migrants 28
Minchin, L. 3, 12, 117, 118
Minster for Employment 163
Morgan, G. 92
Morrey, T. 5
mutual understanding and support 158–9
mystery, menopause as a 21

N

Nash, M. 151
National Association of Schoolmasters/Union
  of Women Teachers 91
National Childhood Development Study
  (NCDS) 6
National Education Union 91
National Institute for Health and Care
  Excellence (NICE) 22, 117
  2015 Guidance 21, 25, 26
National Union of Teachers 96
negative experiences, impact of 57
negative stereotypes 80
Netherlands, the 5, 82
New Reproductive Technologies (NRT) 32
NHS Employers 4
Nokes, C. 3

O

occupational health professionals 56, 79, 92,
  111, 135
occupations, range of 12, 161
oestrogen 24
older workers 20–1, 33, 61, 67–8, 69, 72,
  73, 78, 82, 92, 143
open culture, need for 53
Open University, The 130–1
over-visibilization in workplaces 123

P

Papadatou, A. 94–5
part-time jobs 85
Paul, J. 90, 95
Perz, J. 28
Philippopoulos-Mihalopoulos, A. 12–13,
  116, 119, 121–31

post-menopause 1, 30, 117
precarious jobs 5, 93, 161
premature menopause 2, 15n2, 23, 30–1, 158
private issue, menopause as 96
productivity 7, 26–7, 81, 83, 84–5, 86, 118
Prospect 91, 101–2
psychological contracts 45–6, 60, 68, 69,
  71–3, 84, 158–9
public sector unions 91
Pulignano, V. 92
Putnam, L. 53

R

race 26, 137, 140, 148
reasonable adjustments for menopause
  symptoms 58, 79
recognized the ambivalence involved in
  men using their workplace position to
  challenge power relations 147
remote working 82, 83
reproduction, and menopause 32
request process, right to 71
Riach, K. 3, 5, 6, 58, 95, 110, 119, 131, 161
Roberts, C. 26
role changes 47, 51
Royal College of General Practitioners 3
Royal College of Gynaecologists 3
Royal College of Nurses (RCN) 91, 101

S

Scribner, R.T. 140–1
sectoral skill bodies 4
self-awareness 50
self-help cognitive behaviour therapy 5
self-help texts 24–5
self-identity 143
'Sex, myths and the menopause'
  (documentary) 142
sex hormones 23–4
shared spaces 125, 128
  tensions in 130
  see also workplaces
sick leave 47, 51, 96
sick pay 96, 110
small and medium sized enterprises 6–7, 72
social justice 43, 44, 140, 141, 146
spatial justice 130, 158–9
  and hot flushes at work 121–9
  invisibilization 122
  and lawscapes 13, 122, 123–4, 130–1
  negative effects of injustice 126
  reading of 116
  and tiltedness 128, 129, 130
  and withdrawal 123, 130
Spinoza, B. 121
staff magazine 75
staff-focused approaches 74
Steffan, B. 5
stereotyped 3, 90, 96, 160

Printed and bound by CPI Group (UK) Ltd, Croydon, CR0 4YY

23/04/2025

14661024-0005